Embrace a Biblically Centered Life!

"Wisdom That Transforms. Action That Lasts."

The Get Wisdom Commitment

At Get Wisdom Publishing we believe that true wisdom has the power to transform lives. Our mission is to equip readers with timeless insights and practical tools that inspire growth, guide decisions, and empower purposeful living. We don't just inform—we empower.

Our books combine profound understanding with real-life application, enabling readers to unlock their potential and navigate life's challenges with clarity and confidence. With each step guided by wisdom, we help you create lasting change and live the life you deserve.

When wisdom meets purpose, transformation follows.

Embrace a Biblically Centered Life!

Copyright

The COMMITMENTS of a Jesus Follower: Practical Christian Living and Discipleship, by Stephen H Berkey, published by Get Wisdom Publishing, Box 465, Thompsons Station, TN 37179, copyright © 2024, Stephen H Berkey

All rights reserved. No portion of this book may be reproduced in any form without written permission from the publisher, except as permitted by U.S. copyright law. For permission contact: info@getwisdompublishing.com

Scriptures marked ESV are taken from THE HOLY BIBLE, ENGLISH STANDARD VERSION® Copyright© 2001 by Crossway, a publishing ministry of Good News Publishers. Used by permission.

Scriptures marked NLT are taken from the HOLY BIBLE, NEW LIVING TRANSLATION, copyright© 1996, 2004, 2007 by Tyndale House Foundation. Used by permission of Tyndale House Publishers, Inc., Carol Stream, Illinois 60188. All rights reserved. Used by permission.

Scriptures marked HCSB are taken from the HOLMAN CHRISTIAN STANDARD BIBLE (HCSB): Scripture taken from the HOLMAN CHRISTIAN STANDARD BIBLE, copyright© 1999, 2000, 2002, 2003 by Holman Bible Publishers, Nashville Tennessee. All rights reserved.

Scriptures marked NIV are taken from the NEW INTERNATIONAL VERSION (NIV): Scripture taken from THE HOLY BIBLE, NEW INTERNATIONAL VERSION ®. Copyright© 1973, 1978, 1984, 2011 by Biblica, Inc.™. Used by permission of Zondervan.

ISBN 978-1-952359-75-0   (paperback)
ISBN 978-1-952359-76-7   (kindle)

This book is available as an audiobook on our Amazon Jesus Follower Series page:

Unlock Biblical Wisdom and Transform Your Faith

**For more information
about the Jesus Follower Bible Study Series:**
https://getwisdompublishing.com/jesus-follower-series/

Embrace a Biblically Centered Life!

Jesus Follower Bible Study Series

The COMMITMENTS of a Jesus Follower

Practical Christian Living and Discipleship

Stephen H Berkey

| This book is available as an audiobook on our Amazon Jesus Follower Series page: | |

Embrace a Biblically Centered Life!

Free PDF
Living Wisely

The Life Planning Guide

A Quick-Start Guide to Purposeful Living and Wise Decisions!

Discover the five life domains: purpose, people, principles, productivity, and perspective. Wisdom is the ability to apply truth and logic to real-life decisions and produce good outcomes. It influences your choices and will produce action that lasts. Consider and apply the five practical wisdom principles for daily living. (6 pages)

Free PDF: https://getwisdompublishing.com/resource-registration/

Free PDF

Five Practical Principles For Life

When wisdom meets purpose, transformation follows.

Embrace a Biblically Centered Life!

Free PDF
Wise Decision-Making
[Get the ebook version for 99 cents]

You can make good choices.

This free resource provides a project-oriented perspective and gives ten detailed steps to analyze issues/problems to determine a solution. (26 pages)

Good decisions expand your horizons. Don't allow the fear of decision-making paralyze your ability to make good choices. Think through the reasonable alternatives and move forward. When your eyes are on the goal, making good decisions is easier.

Free PDF: https://getwisdompublishing.com/resource-registration/

Kindle ebook for 99 cents: https://www.amazon.com/dp/B09SYGWRVL/

Ebook

Free PDF

Make Thoughtful Decisions!

Good decisions expand your horizons.

Embrace a Biblically Centered Life!

The Jesus Follower Journey
The Jesus Follower Study Series

The Jesus Follower Bible Study Series will provide you with a complete description of the nature, characteristics, obligations, commitments, and responsibilities of a true Jesus follower.

Go to our Amazon Book Series page for your copy:
https://www.amazon.com/dp/B0DHP39P5J

The RELATIONSHIP CHARACTERISTICS of a Jesus Follower:
  Are you right with God?
The ONE ANOTHER INSTRUCTIONS to a Jesus Follower:
  Are you right with one another?
The WORSHIP of a Jesus Follower:
  Is your worship acceptable or in vain?
The PRAYER of a Jesus Follower:
  What Scripture says about unleashing the power of God.
The DANGERS of SIN for a Jesus Follower:
  God HATES sin! He abhors sin!
The FOCUS for a Jesus Follower:
  Keep your eyes fixed on Jesus!
The HEART Requirements of a Jesus Follower:
  Follow with all your heart, mind, body, and soul!
The COMMITMENTS of a Jesus Follower:
  Practical Christian living and discipleship.
The OBEDIENCE Requirements for a Jesus Follower:
  Ignore at your own risk!

A related book to this series is, *Effective Life Change: Applying Biblical Wisdom to Live Your Best Life!* This book offers a practical and powerful guide to help navigate life's challenges based on the proverbial wisdom of the Bible. It offers ten commitments that will profoundly change your life.

Effective Life Change
Applying Biblical Wisdom to Live Your Best Life!

Why Read This Book?

- Transform Your life with Biblical Wisdom.
- Cultivate Practical Wisdom in Your life.
- Navigate Life with a Perspective on Biblical Truth.
- Unlock the Proverbs of the Bible to Live Your Best Life.
- Change and Transform Your life.

Practical Application: These aren't theology or religious discussions, they're practical tools for everyday living.

Get Your Copy Today!

https://www.amazon.com/dp/1952359732
Available in Hardcover, Paperback, Kindle, and Audiobook.

Table of Contents

Free PDFs Living Wisely and Wise Decision-Making 4

Message From the Author 9

Introduction 12

Lesson 1 Being A Committed Disciple 15

Lesson 2 Total Commitment 31

Lesson 3 Choose Enduring Faith 48

Lesson 4 Lordship, Surrender, and Submission 59

Lesson 5 Take Up Your CROSS 73

Lesson 6 Be a Living Sacrifice 84

Lesson 7 Commit To Spiritual Growth 96

Lesson 8 Serve Others and Produce Fruit 115

Lesson 9 Reject Worldly Values 129

Lesson 10 Persevere and Stand Firm 144

Transformation Road Map 160

Leader Guide 162

Appendix A We Reap What We Sow! 177

Free PDF MAKE WISE DECISIONS 178

Free PDF Life Improvement Principles 179

What Next? 180

The OBSCURE Bible Study Series 181

Life Planning Series 182

Personal Daily Prayer Guide 183

Notes 184

About the Author 185

Message From the Author

Dear Fellow Christ follower,

Welcome to a journey of faith and discovery.

As the author of this Bible study series, I am excited about the future because I believe this book provides the potential to transform lives, deepen our understanding of God's Word, and ignite a desire within us—a fire that draws us into the presence of our God.

Why read the Jesus Follower Series?

Deeper Roots: We all long for roots that run deep—roots anchored in truth, love, and purpose. In this series, we'll dig into the bedrock of Scripture, unearthing spiritual principles that will guide us in our faith journey.

Authentic Discipleship: Being a Jesus follower isn't about rituals or a superficial commitment. It's about walking the narrow path, picking up your cross, and living a life that loves God, follows Jesus, and loves one another. We will explore what it means to be authentic disciples.

Unveiling Mysteries: God is a source of mysteries and His Word is waiting to be discovered. Together we will examine and encounter the living Word—the One who breathes life into every syllable.

Community and Connection: We are not meant to walk this path alone. As you read, imagine joining a global community of fellow seekers. We will discuss, question, and grow together. Our shared journey will enrich us all. I encourage you to gather friends to join you in this journey.

Expected Benefits:

Renewed Passion: Prepare yourself to wake up each morning with a renewed passion for God's Word. These studies will ignite your hunger for truth and draw you into deeper relationship with the Author of Life.

Practical Application: These aren't theoretical discussions; they're practical tools for everyday living. Expect to see real-life changes—whether it's in your relationships, commitment, or prayer life.

Spiritual Resilience: Life's storms will come, but armed with the insights from God's Word, you can stand firm. Your faith will weather trials, doubts, and uncertainties. You will emerge stronger and more resilient.

Joyful Obedience: As we explore the nature of discipleship, you'll discover that obedience isn't a burden—it's a joy. The path of obedience leads to peace, and you'll find yourself saying, "Yes, Lord!" with newfound delight.

Let's Begin!

So, turn the page. Dive into the first chapter. Let the words seep into your soul. And remember, you're not alone—we're on this pilgrimage together. May these books be more than ink on paper; may they be stepping stones toward a life that leads to eternity. Amen!

"We believe applied wisdom empowers life change. Our books provide clarity, inspiration, and tools to equip readers to live their best life."

Embrace a Biblically Centered Life!

My prayer is that you will

Be tenacious like Job
Walk like Enoch
Believe like Abraham
Wrestle like Jacob
Dress like Joseph
Lead like Moses
Conquer like Deborah
Be fearless like Shamgar
Inspire like Josuha
Influence like Esther
Dance like David
Ask like Jabez
Have the faith of Daniel
Pray like Elijah
Trust like Elisha
Commit like Isaiah
Be courageous like Benaiah
Rebuild like Nehemiah
Be obedient like Hosea
Be zealous like Zacchaeus
Surrender like Mary
Stand firm like Stephen
Speak like Peter
Seize opportunities like Philip
Submit like Paul
Overcome like the Elect (Saints)
Worship like the 24 Elders
and
Love like Jesus

Steve

Introduction

Book Description

Are you ready to embark on a journey of faith that goes beyond the surface? Do you yearn to experience a life fully committed to Jesus in every aspect? *The COMMITMENTS of a Jesus Follower: Practical Christian Living and Discipleship* offers a roadmap to transform your spiritual walk from ordinary to extraordinary.

This Bible study unveils the essential commitments required to truly follow Jesus and live a life that reflects His love and purpose. Through ten profound and practical lessons, you'll discover how to:

Build a Rock-Solid Foundation: Understand and embrace the core principles that form the bedrock of your faith, enabling you to stand firm in your commitment to Christ.

Embrace Total Surrender: Learn the transformative power of living under the Lordship of Jesus, submitting to His guidance and will.

Embrace Unyielding Faith: Develop a faith that not only endures but thrives amidst life's trials and uncertainties, anchoring you in God's promises.

Reject Worldly Allure: Cultivate a heart that seeks after God's kingdom, producing lasting fruit and rejecting the temporary values of the world.

Persevere and Stand Firm: Gain the resilience and strength to face challenges with unwavering courage and steadfastness, standing firm in your faith.

Each lesson is deeply rooted in Scripture and packed with practical insights, real-life applications, and thought-provoking questions designed to challenge and inspire you. Whether you are a new believer looking to grow in your faith or a seasoned disciple seeking a deeper relationship with Christ, this study provides the tools and encouragement you need to live with purpose, courage, and unwavering faith.

In addition, you'll explore themes such as:

Being a Committed Disciple: What does it mean to follow Jesus wholeheartedly and what is the transformative impact on your life? You will learn the importance of giving your all to Jesus and discover the blessings that come from such devotion.

Enduring Faith: How do you maintain strong faith in the face of trials, doubts, and uncertainties? How does it strengthen your relationship with God? Your faith walk is a continuous journey of growing in your faith, deepening your understanding of God's Word.

Lordship: Understanding the significance of living under Jesus' lordship and the freedom found in following His will. You will be encouraged to embrace lifestyle of commitments, reflecting Jesus' love and compassion to those around you.

Producing Fruit: You will experience the joy and fulfillment of serving others while meeting the needs of those less fortunate.

Rejecting Worldly Values: How do you stay focused on eternal values and live counter-culturally in a world that often contradicts biblical principles?

Perseverance and Standing Firm: You will learn the importance of perseverance in your faith journey and how to remain steadfast in the face of challenges.

This Bible study is not just about gaining knowledge; it's about experiencing real-life transformation. Through practical applications and reflective questions you'll be challenged and equipped to live a life fully committed to your faith.

Don't settle for a superficial relationship! Take the next step in your spiritual journey and discover the joy and fulfillment of living fully committed to Him.

Are you ready to say "yes" to the call of true discipleship?

Group Discussion or Individual Study

These studies can be done individually or in a small discussion group. An important value of the study is in the discussion questions. We all see life differently and the thoughts and ideas shared in a group will often lead to a richer understanding of the Scripture. We recommend doing these studies in a group, if possible.

Format of Lessons

The format of the lessons is not the same in each book. We chose a format that best fit the material.

Focused Biblical Wisdom.
Everyday Faith Application!

Lesson 1
Being A Committed Disciple

"The greatest tragedy in life is not unanswered prayer, but unoffered prayer. The greatest tragedy is not that we are not committed disciples, but that we are not fully committed to being disciples of Jesus."
John Stott

We have covered the subjects of loving God, loving one another, and making disciples in other books in this Series. Thus, we will generally ignore these topics in this book. They certainly qualify as commitments for a Jesus follower but because they are discussed elsewhere, we will focus on nine other important commitments that a disciple or follower would emphasize in order to please God. Pleasing God reflects a heart aligned with His will and purpose.

HOW DO WE PLEASE GOD?

Overview

Living to please God is a mark of true discipleship. Rather than conforming to worldly desires or seeking human approval, disciples are called to live in a way that honors God and reflects His holiness. This focus requires aligning our actions and character with His will. Pleasing God is not merely about external behavior, but rather it flows from an inner heart committed to Christ. As believers grow spiritually they seek to please God by avoiding sin and pursuing righteousness.

Pleasing God involves a life of obedience and service to others. It may also include sacrificial acts that reflect Christ's love. Commitment to God's purposes, such as acts of compassion, generosity, and humility, are common characteristics of a committed disciple who wants to please God.

Faith is also fundamental in pleasing God. Without faith, it is impossible to please Him. Faith enables believers to rely on God's guidance and wisdom, trusting Him in all aspects of life.

The Bible tells us a number of key characteristics for pleasing God. We will review nine ways the Bible speaks of pleasing God:

1. FAITH: Hebrews 11:6 *And without faith, it is impossible to please God, because anyone who comes to him must believe that he exists and that he rewards those who earnestly seek him.* NIV

This verse highlights that faith is essential in pleasing God. Faith acknowledges God's presence and actively seeks a relationship with Him.

2. LIVING SACRIFICE: Romans 12:1-2 *Therefore, I urge you, brothers and sisters, in view of God's mercy, to offer your bodies as a living sacrifice, holy and pleasing to God—this is your true and proper worship. Do not conform to the pattern of this world, but be transformed by the renewing of your mind.* NIV

Paul urges believers to be a living sacrifice as an act of worship. Transformation through a renewed mind aligns believers' lives with what is pleasing to God.

3. SPIRTUAL GROWTH: 1 Thessalonians 4:1 *As for other matters, brothers and sisters, we instructed you how to live in order to please God, as in fact you are living. Now we ask you and urge you in the Lord Jesus to do this more and more.* NIV

Paul encourages the Thessalonians to continue their spiritual growth in ways that please Him, indicating that pleasing God is an ongoing pursuit involving obedience.

4. BEARING FRUIT: Colossians 1:10 *So as to walk in a manner worthy of the Lord, fully <u>pleasing to him</u>, bearing fruit in every good work and increasing in the knowledge of God.* ESV

This verse indicates we can please Him by bearing fruit and growing in the knowledge of God. Paul is telling the Colossians that pleasing God is tied to <u>active</u> spiritual growth.

5. GOD's APPROVAL: Galatians 1:10 *Am I now trying to win the approval of human beings, or of God? Or am I trying to please people? If I were still trying to please people, I would not be a servant of Christ.* NIV

Paul contrasts pleasing people with pleasing God, underscoring that a disciple's focus should be on God's approval, not human approval.

6. EDURING PURPOSE: 2 Corinthians 5:9 *So we make it our goal to <u>please him</u>, whether we are at home in the body or away from it.* NIV

God is to be the central goal of our life, whether in this life or in the next. It is an enduring purpose for every believer.

7. SHUN EVIL WAYS: Ephesians 5:10-14 *Carefully determine what <u>pleases the Lord</u>. 11 Take no part in the worthless deeds of evil and darkness; instead, expose them. 12 It is shameful even to talk about the things that ungodly people do in secret. 13 But their evil intentions will be exposed when the light shines on them, 14 for the light makes everything visible.* NLT

Paul tells the Ephesians to avoid evil and even to expose people who are involved in evil and worthless activities. Goodness and light will expose evil intentions and deeds.

8. BEING A WITNESS: 1 Thessalonians 2:4 *but just as we have been approved by God to be entrusted with the gospel, so we speak, not to please man, but to <u>please God</u> who tests our hearts.* ESV

We are to speak and proclaim the gospel because it has been approved and tested by God.

9. BE GOOD AND KIND: Hebrews 13:16 *Do not neglect to do good and to share what you have, for such sacrifices are <u>pleasing to God</u>.* ESV

We must not neglect good deeds because good works are pleasing to God. What we do matters to Him.

DISCUSSION QUESTIONS: Pleasing God

1. Did Jesus please God based on the following?
Matthew 3:17 *and behold, a voice from heaven said, "This is my beloved Son, with whom I am well pleased.* ESV
John 8:29 *And he who sent me is with me. He has not left me alone, for I always do the things that are pleasing to him.* ESV

2. Look up the following passages and identify what kinds of things please God?

Romans 12:1 _____
Romans 14:17 _____
Philippians 4:18 _____
Colossians 1:10 _____
Colossians 3:20 _____
Hebrews 11:6 _____
Hebrews 12:28 _____
Hebrews 13:21 _____
Galatians 1:10 _____
1 Thessalonians 2:4 _____
1 John 3:22 _____
1 Timothy 2:2-3 _____
1 Timothy 5:4 _____

3. How do we please God based on the following passages?

Romans 14:23   _____
John 15:5   _____
Galatians 2:20   _____
1 Corinthians 15:10 _____

4. Based on the following, how can pleasing God by obedience lead us through a path of suffering?

Philippians 1:29-30 *For it has been granted to you that for the sake of Christ you should not only believe in him but also suffer for his sake, 30 engaged in the same conflict that you saw I had and now hear that I still have.* ESV

1 Peter 2:19-21 *For this is a gracious thing, when, mindful of God, one endures sorrows while suffering unjustly. 20 For what credit is it if, when you sin and are beaten for it, you endure? But if when you do good and suffer for it you endure, this is a gracious thing in the sight of God.* ESV

SUMMARY: Pleasing God

Pleasing God is a defining commitment of a true disciple's life. It involves sacrificial living and spiritual growth, as well as dedication to God's purposes. Disciples are called to continually seek God's will, relying on the Holy Spirit to help them live a life that reflects His holiness and love. God is not demanding perfection but rather a faithful pursuit of His heart and purpose for our lives.

Philippians 2:12-13 *Dear friends, you always followed my instructions when I was with you. And now that I am away, it is even more important. Work hard to show the results of your salvation, obeying God with deep reverence and fear. 13 For*

God is working in you, giving you the desire and the power to do what pleases him. NLT

Working out our salvation is fulfilling God's purpose for our lives. God enables believers to live in a way that is pleasing to Him. Discipleship is a cooperative effort between believers and the Holy Spirit working within us.

THE CALL TO FOLLOW JESUS

Our call to follow Jesus is more than simply having faith and belief: we are to be followers or disciples. We are also called to love others while serving Christ. We are to grow and exercise our spiritual gifts to build up the church while personally exhibiting the fruit of the Spirit (Gal 5:22). Jesus wants to transform us from sinful people driven by worldly values to spiritual disciples dedicated to the ways of God.

In Mark 1:17 Jesus says to follow Him in order to be fishers of men and Luke tells us to be a living witness to the dying world around us. Luke makes it more personal when he says that we are to take up our cross in order to follow Him (Luke 9:23).

The result of following is that we become a new creation. We have a new identity in Christ Jesus that is driven by God's will in our lives (2 Corinthians 5:17).

WHAT DOES IT MEAN TO BE A DISCIPLE?

There are a number of acceptable definitions for a Christian disciple. For our purposes we will define a disciple as follows:

> A disciple is a person growing in his or her _relationship_ with Christ Jesus, who is eager to _learn and apply_ the truth of the Word of God in his or her life, resulting in a deeper commitment to a _Christ-like lifestyle_ and service.

Obviously if you are a true disciple you are saved. But it does not mean that simply because you are saved, you are a disciple. You may be only a member, participant, or even just a fan.

Based on this definition, if you are a committed disciple you are meeting three essential requirements:

1. You have a *growing relationship* with Christ.
2. You are *learning and actively growing* in your faith.
3. You are *experiencing a transformative commitment* to a Christ-like lifestyle.

There are two important keys in this definition. The first is the commitment to a Christ-like lifestyle. This can be summed up by two concepts:

The first key is obedience – and that may be the most important one. Obedience to God's Word must be a desire in your life, and you must be open to the leading of the Holy Spirit.

You might describe this using other words, but it boils down to obedience. Our problems began in the Garden of Eden because Adam and Eve rebelled against God. Think about it! What couldn't or wouldn't be solved if we simply obeyed God's Word? Remember, John reported that Jesus said, *"If you keep my commandments, you will abide in my love, just as I have kept my Father's commandments and abide in his love."* (John 15:10 ESV). So it's obvious the intent is that we walk in His ways.

The second key is whether we are really seeking the presence of God in our lives. Are we seeking Him with all our heart? David is a good example. He did some terrible things — serious sin. Yet, God loved David. Do you remember why? David was a man who *sought after the heart of God* (1 Samuel 13:14), even though he was sinful like all other followers.

The question for you today is:
Am I seeking after the heart of God?

A disciple is a Christian in process. As long as we keep learning and growing in Christ we are on the right path. We must continue to say "yes" to God in order to grow into His likeness. We must allow ourselves to be used by God for His purposes.

COMMITMENT

Webster's Dictionary generically defines a disciple as a pupil who accepts and assists in spreading the doctrines of another. But it also says that a disciple was one of the twelve Apostles of Jesus. Today, a Christian disciple is generally considered to be a person who believes in Jesus Christ and who is growing in his or her faith.

Let's examine in more depth how the Bible describes a disciple's commitment.

> *"If anyone comes to me and does not hate his father and mother, his wife and children, his brothers and sisters – yes, even his own life – he cannot be my disciple. And anyone who does not carry his cross and follow me cannot be my disciple . . . In the same way, any of you who does not give up everything he has cannot be my disciple.*
> (Luke 14:26-27, 33 NIV)

The term "hate" in this verse should be understood in light of Genesis 29:30-31, which means to "love less." Jesus does not advocate animosity but rather a supreme allegiance to Him that transcends even family relationships.

Commitment is a foundational characteristic for being a disciple! It means we make a commitment to Christ and to a Christ-like lifestyle. When you begin studying the Bible you may have questions like:

- What does it mean to take up my cross?
- Am I going to experience persecution?
- Must I give up all my possessions?
- How do I make Jesus the center of my life?
- Do I have to give up everything?

You may see these issues and other challenges when reading portions of Scripture. Maybe in some circumstances they apply, but in most of our lives, we are not talking about the extremes of the Christian walk. Yes, God must come first in our lives and we must be committed to Him. Commitment means more than just giving lip service to our beliefs — it also involves actions.

But the fundamental nature of the attitude and commitment is that it is to be a relationship. We develop a bond of love, loyalty, and dedication to Jesus and our faith. We exhibit hope and live a life of peace because we know the end of the story.

Along the way the question may arise as to whether faith, hope, and love drive our lives (1 Corinthians 13: 13). At the end of the love chapter in 1 Corinthians 13:13 (NLT) Paul concludes: *Three things will last forever—faith, hope, and love—and the greatest of these is love.* Thus, an important concept for disciples committed to following the teachings of Christ is that they should not be following rules routinely, but living a life that expresses a deep and personal devotion to God.

It is important to recognize that love is the foundation of our obedience and loyalty. We do good works because of our love for God and what He has done for us, not because we are under some obligation to perform good deeds. Love should be the foundation of all we do, whether it is toward God or our neighbor:

> **Matthew 22:37-40** *Jesus replied, You must love the LORD your God with all your heart, all your soul, and all your mind. 38 This is the first and greatest commandment. 39 A second is equally important: Love your neighbor as yourself. 40 The entire law and all the demands of the prophets are based on these two commandments.* NLT

OTHER BIBLICAL REQUIREMENTS

In addition, there are other passages that outline a number of actions associated with being a disciple.

Abide in Prayer: A disciple abides with Jesus and is rewarded with answered prayer. A disciple prays for himself, family, and friends. Jesus said:

> *If you abide in me, and my words abide in you, ask whatever you wish, and it will be done for you. 8 By this my Father is glorified, that you bear much fruit and so prove to be my disciples.* (John 15:7-8 ESV)

Bear Fruit: A disciple is expected to grow in the knowledge of God being transformed into the likeness of Christ resulting in performing good deeds and having a godly character.

> *By this is my Father glorified, that you bear much fruit, and [so] prove to be my disciples.* (John 15:8 ESV)

Have a Purpose: A disciple needs to know and understand what they believe.

> *Always be prepared to give an answer to everyone who asks you to give the reason for the hope that you have. But do this with gentleness and respect.* (1 Peter 3:15 NIV)

Grow in Knowledge: A disciple is continually growing in his or her knowledge of Christ.

> *But grow in the grace and knowledge of our Lord and Savior Jesus Christ. . .* (2 Peter 3:18 NIV)

Know the Word of God: A disciple lives a lifestyle characterized by the Word of God.

> *Let the word of Christ dwell in you richly as you teach and admonish one another with all wisdom . . .*
> (Colossians 3:16-17 NIV)

> *All Scripture is God-breathed and is useful for teaching, rebuking, correcting and training in righteousness, so that the man of God may be thoroughly equipped for every good work.* (2 Timothy 3:16-17 NIV)

Serve Others: A disciple uses his or her gifts, skills and talents to serve others and support the local church. Disciples are people of action – they do something!

> *Each one should use whatever gift he has received to serve others, faithfully administering God's grace in its various forms.* (1 Peter 4:10 NIV)

> *Whatever you have learned or received or heard from me, or seen in me-- put it into practice. And the God of peace will be with you.* (Philippians 4:9 NIV)

Be Connected: A disciple is connected to the church and Christian community through significant relationships.

> *Every day they [the early Christians] continued to meet together in the temple courts. They broke bread in their homes and ate together with glad and sincere hearts, praising God and enjoying the favor of all the people . . .* (Acts 2:46-47 NIV)

Guard Your Speech: A disciple is careful about his or her speech.

> *Let your conversation be always full of grace, seasoned with salt, so that you may know how to answer everyone.* (Colossians 4:6 NIV)

Persevere: A disciple will not only teach and mentor others, he will share his struggles.

> *You, however, know all about my teaching, my way of life, my purpose, faith, patience, love, endurance, persecutions, sufferings – what kinds of things happened to me. . . Yet the Lord rescued me from all of them.* (2 Timothy 3:10-11 NIV)

Do Good Deeds: A disciple is called to love and perform good deeds while encouraging one another.

> And let us consider how to stir up one another to love and good works, 25 not neglecting to meet together, as is the habit of some, but encouraging one another, and all the more as you see the Day drawing near. (Hebrews 10:24-25 ESV)

Encourage Others: A disciple will be an encouragement to others, particularly to the body of Christ.

> For you know that we dealt with each of you as a father deals with his own children, encouraging, comforting and urging you to live lives worthy of God, who calls you into his kingdom and glory. (1Thessalonians 2:11-12 NIV)

These Biblical teachings make it clear that being a disciple involves action and being intentional. We can't consider ourselves a disciple if we are not actively participating in our faith and the faith community. We should be developing and growing in our relationship with the Lord Jesus Christ, learning from the Word of God, and committed to living a Christian lifestyle. We do that by reading and studying the Bible, praying regularly, attending worship services faithfully, being connected to a local church congregation or small group, and serving others in some way.

Finally we must understand that real commitment is our response to what God/Jesus did for us. It's not a means to earn favor or salvation but a response to the grace we've received. Remember in 1 John 4:19 we are told that Jesus loved us first, therefore, we should love Him and others like He loved us.

EXERCISE: In the following passages describe what you believe would be <u>expected</u> from a committed disciple.

1. Hold on to the Vine.
John 15:1-8 *I am the true vine, and my Father is the vinedresser. 2 Every branch of mine that does not bear fruit he takes away, and every branch that does bear fruit he prunes, that it may bear more fruit. 3 Already you are clean because of the word that I have spoken to you. 4 Abide in me, and I in you. As the*

branch cannot bear fruit by itself, unless it abides in the vine, neither can you, unless you abide in me. 5 I am the vine; you are the branches. Whoever abides in me and I in him, he it is that bears much fruit, for apart from me you can do nothing. 6 If anyone does not abide in me he is thrown away like a branch and withers; and the branches are gathered, thrown into the fire, and burned. 7 If you abide in me, and my words abide in you, ask whatever you wish, and it will be done for you. 8 By this my Father is glorified, that you bear much fruit and so prove to be my disciples. ESV

2. Fear God and keep His commandments

Ecclesiastes 12:13-14 *The end of the matter; all has been heard. Fear God and keep his commandments, for this is the whole duty of man. 14 For God will bring every deed into judgment, with every secret thing, whether good or evil.* ESV

3. Total Allegiance and priority.

Mark 10:21 *And Jesus, looking at him, loved him, and said to him, "You lack one thing: go, sell all that you have and give to the poor, and you will have treasure in heaven; and come, follow me." ESV*

4. Guard your hearts (inner self).

Proverbs 4:23 *Guard your heart above all else, for it determines the course of your life. NLT*

Philippians 4:7 *And the peace of God, which surpasses all understanding, will guard your hearts and your minds in Christ Jesus. ESV*

Matthew 15:18-19 *But what comes out of the mouth proceeds from the heart, and this defiles a person. ESV*

5. Be alert, stand firm

1 Corinthians 16:13-14 *Be on guard. Stand firm in the faith. Be courageous. Be strong. 14 And do everything with love. NLT*

CONCLUSION

If you are a disciple or one considering a commitment, what does it mean to you to be totally committed? What would it look like in your life? The following might be some expectations:

- Be in church every Sunday.
- Have a daily quiet time.
- Be involved with some ministry or service.
- Being one of the spiritual leaders in my family.
- Walk in the ways of the Lord (live obediently).
- Grow in my knowledge of God and His truth.
- Tithing and giving offerings above my tithe (generousity).
- Sharing my faith with others.

These commitments require r*egular self-examination and dependence on the power and leading of the Holy Spirit.* Ongoing repentance and renewal is often necessary along with accountability in your faith walk.

Success in these commitments will come through God's grace, not human effort. Growth will be progressive and experience hills and valleys – instant perfection does not occur. Community support will be critical to success. This is not something that can be done alone or in isolation. It will require constant attention.

DISCUSSION AND THOUGHT QUESTIONS

1. What do you think Jesus meant when He said, "If anyone would come after me, let him deny himself and take up his cross daily and follow me" (Luke 9:23)?

2. How does your commitment to Christ influence your daily decisions, relationships, and use of resources?

3. What are the biggest challenges or obstacles you face in maintaining wholehearted commitment to following Jesus in today's culture?

4. How do you distinguish between authentic commitment to Christ and merely going through religious motions?

5. What specific practices or habits have helped you grow and maintain your commitment as a disciple?

6. How has your understanding of what it means to be a committed disciple changed or deepened over time? Reflect on your spiritual journey and recognize growth in your understanding of discipleship.

Wisdom to Action
Challenge

What specific area of your life do you need to surrender more fully to Christ this week? How can you demonstrate your love for God through obedience in this area?

Lesson 2
Total Commitment

*Whatever you do, work at it with all your heart,
as working for the Lord, not for human masters.*
Colossians 3:23 NIV

INTRODUCTION

We discussed commitment in Lesson 1 as part of describing what is required or expected from a disciple of Christ. In this lesson we will take a deeper look into the meaning and implications of making a serious commitment to Christ. Is it simply a matter of belief and commitment or do other commands or instructions come into play? Is "absolute obedience" necessary?

To be a committed disciple of Christ is to embrace a life of devotion and transformation. Jesus invites all who follow Him to deny themselves, take up their cross daily, and walk in His footsteps (Luke 9:23). This call is not for the faint of heart but for those wanting to give their heart and soul to loving and serving God. Commitment is not an option for a serious follower of Jesus. Commitment is the hallmark of true discipleship, reflecting a life fully aligned with God's will and purpose.

Commitment to Christ involves three key dimensions: identity, priorities, and actions.

1. **Identity**: Committed disciples find their identity in Jesus. They are no longer defined by worldly standards but by their relationship with Jesus. This identity as a child of God (Galatians 3:26) transforms personal values, worldview, and life purpose.

2. **Priorities**: Jesus becomes the central reality of a disciple's faith. Earthly pursuits are secondary to the needs of the kingdom of God (Matthew 6:33). Disciples willingly count the cost of following Jesus (Luke 14:28-33), knowing that the eternal rewards far surpass any earthly difficulties or sacrifices.

3. **Actions**: A disciple's faith is expressed in obedience to God's commands and the teachings of Christ. This means commitment is:

   - Loving God and others with all our heart (Matthew 22:37-39).
   - Bearing fruit through abiding in Christ (John 15:4-5).
   - Living sacrificially by presenting our lives as a living sacrifice, holy and, pleasing to God (Romans 12:1).
   - Engaging in ministry and mission, sharing the gospel and making disciples of all nations (Matt 28:19-20).

Being a fully committed disciple is not about perfection but about purpose and intent. It is a life continually being conformed to the image of Christ as the disciple works out his salvation. It is marked by obedience, trust, humility, perseverance, and love.

ALLEGIANCE: Take Up Your Cross

Luke 14:26-27, 33
If anyone comes to me and does not hate father and mother, wife and children, brothers and sisters—yes, even their own life—such a person cannot be my disciple. And whoever does not carry their cross and follow me cannot be my disciple . . . In the same way, those of you who do not give up everything you have cannot be my disciples. NIV

Commitment to Jesus requires prioritizing Him above all other relationships including family. This passage delivers a profound call to discipleship, underscoring the radical and transformative commitment required to follow Jesus. These verses emphasize that discipleship requires self-denial and a <u>willingness</u> to renounce worldly possessions. This reflects the depth of devotion necessary to walk in His footsteps. In essence it means that Jesus is the number one priority in your life.

The call to "carry your cross" expands the demand for prioritizing Jesus. In Jesus' time the cross symbolized suffering, humiliation, and death. For His followers, this phrase signified a willingness to endure rejection, hardship, and even death for His sake. Discipleship is not a casual commitment but a wholehearted decision to embrace Christ's mission.

This does not mean a disciple does not love and care for others and their family. The issue is priority! Jesus must be number one in your life. If that is true then family will be loved better than if you did not follow Christ.

Jesus sets forth a vision of discipleship characterized by *radical commitment*. The use of the word "hate" is not literal but an idiom emphasizing the necessity of loving Christ more than family or self. This radical supreme loyalty demands reordering life priorities. and placing Christ above all other cherished earthly bonds. For Chicago Cubs fans this means Jesus is number one and the Cubs are number two. ☺

By urging followers to "carry their cross" the call for allegiance is colored by a scarlet stain. This phrase signifies embracing self-denial, accepting potential suffering, and aligning fully with Christ's mission, even at great personal cost. In verse 33 Jesus broadens the scope, calling disciples to renounce all possessions. This renunciation *symbolizes* total reliance on God and a life oriented toward eternal values rather than material gain. Together, these verses declare that following Jesus reshapes every aspect of life and requires whole-hearted commitment. How could it be any different?

Modern Readers

For Jesus' original audience, His words carried weight in a *collectivist society* where family and community ties defined identity and security. Choosing to follow Jesus often meant the possibility of severing these bonds, leading to social isolation, economic loss, and even persecution. In this historical context His call resonated as both a challenge and an invitation to embrace a greater eternal purpose.

In first-century Jewish culture, family loyalty shaped the order of life. Choosing allegiance to Jesus over family would have been a shocking and countercultural demand, often resulting in ostracism. Jesus' words challenged listeners to reorient their lives around His mission, even when it conflicted with societal norms or familial expectations.

In today's modern society Jesus' words confront cultural tendencies toward materialism, individualism, and comfortable cost-free expressions of faith. It is in stark contrast to those who put self above all else. His demand for a countercultural all-encompassing commitment calls believers to reassess their priorities. A disciple may need to break attachments to possessions or embrace a faith that can transform every aspect of their lives.

Jesus' call to love Him above all else pushes believers to evaluate where their true loyalties lie and challenges the illusion that life can be fulfilled apart from Him.

Remember, the term "hate" means to "love less." Jesus does not advocate animosity but rather a supreme allegiance to Him.

Alignment with New Testament Teachings

This passage aligns easily with broader New Testament teachings on discipleship. For instance, Matthew 16:24-25 echoes the call to self-denial and cross-bearing, while Philippians 3:7-8 reflects Paul's perspective on valuing Christ above all else. These teachings consistently emphasize that true discipleship means sacrifice and prioritizing the eternal over the temporal. They challenge the cultural belief that faith can be convenient and without cost. They remind believers that following Jesus can be transformative, but there are demands and requirements.

In Luke 9:23-24, Jesus reiterates the call to self-denial and cross-bearing. John 12:25 declares, "Anyone who loves their life will lose it, while anyone who hates their life in this world will keep it for eternal life." These passages consistently highlight the sacrificial nature of discipleship and the eternal rewards for prioritizing Christ above all. They contrast sharply with cultural expectations of a convenient or cost-free faith. Instead, they portray discipleship as demanding a radical reorientation of one's values in order to achieve transformation.

Transformative Implications

Embracing this teaching will reorient a believer's relationship with Christ, moving it from superficial to transformative discipleship. It compels followers to evaluate their priorities and live in full dependence on God. This radical commitment fosters spiritual growth and deepens intimacy with Christ.

By taking up one's cross and rejecting worldly possessions, believers embody the heart of true discipleship. This profound commitment not only transforms individual believers but also serves as a powerful testimony to the world of the power of wholehearted devotion to Jesus.

DISCUSSION QUESTIONS

1. What does Jesus mean by "hating" family and life itself? How does this challenge your current priorities?

2. What personal sacrifices have you made (or might you need to make) to follow Jesus fully?

3. What does "taking up your cross" look like in today's world?

4. How does the call to renounce possessions work in a culture of consumerism?

ALLEGIANCE: Be Worthy of Christ
Matthew 10:37-39
"Anyone who loves their father or mother more than me is not worthy of me; anyone who loves their son or daughter more than me is not worthy of me. Whoever does not take up their cross and follow me is not worthy of me. Whoever finds their life will lose it, and whoever loses their life for my sake will find it."
NIV

Allegiance to Christ surpasses family ties and personal ambitions. Matthew 10:37-39 presents a profound call to discipleship that demands supreme allegiance to Jesus. This passage is very similar to Luke 14 above. It challenges believers to embrace a life of self-denial and surrender in order to discover true life.

Jesus declares that anyone who loves their family more than Him is "not worthy" of Him. This stark statement emphasizes that discipleship requires prioritizing Jesus over even the closest human relationships. Far from advocating neglect or disdain for family, Jesus calls simply for a <u>reordering</u> of affections, placing Him at the center of one's life.

The paradox in the last verse further describes this radical commitment: "Whoever finds their life will lose it, and whoever loses their life for my sake will find it." This means that true life is not found in preserving one's own ambitions or comforts but in surrendering them to follow Jesus. Only by losing one's life in service and allegiance to Christ can one experience the fullness of life that He offers.

Several phrases in this passage require careful interpretation:

- *"Not worthy of me"* (v. 37): This phrase reflects the high cost of discipleship. It does not imply exclusion but stresses the necessity of prioritizing Jesus above all other commitments.

- *"Take up your cross"* (v. 38): This is not merely a call to endure life's difficulties but a conscious choice to identify with Christ's mission and to accept the suffering or loss that <u>may</u> accompany it.

- *"Finds his life...loses it"* (v. 39 here and also in Luke 14 passage): This paradox challenges conventional wisdom. It reveals that clinging to earthly priorities leads to spiritual loss, while surrendering those priorities for Christ's sake brings life.

Transformative Implications

Embracing the demands of Matthew 10:37-39 will transform a believer's relationship with Christ. By placing Jesus above all, believers experience a deeper intimacy with Him and a clearer sense of purpose. Redefining priorities fosters a life oriented toward eternal values rather than earthly ones.

DISCUSSION QUESTIONS

5. How have you experienced the paradox of "losing your life" for Christ and finding it?

6. Why is understanding the cost of discipleship important before committing to follow Jesus?

7. How does this passage challenge modern cultural values of self-promotion and comfort?

IMPLICATIONS

What does all this mean for a disciple?

- **Priorities must be reevaluated**: We should regularly assess whether Jesus holds the highest place in our life Is He above relationships, ambitions, and possessions?

- **We must embrace self-denial**: We should practice habits like fasting, sacrificial giving, or volunteering in order to cultivate selflessness and focus on Christ.

- **We should live with eternal perspective**: We should make decisions based on eternal significance rather than on temporary gains in earthly comforts.

- **We should be a witness**: We should demonstrate our faith commitment through actions that reflect Christ's love and priorities.

- **We should strengthen and encourage one another**: We should join a group of believers to support and encourage one another in the challenges of living out total commitment.

FIT FOR SERVICE

Luke 9:62
"No one who puts a hand to the plow and looks back is fit for service in the kingdom of God." NIV

This verse suggests that there is no room for divided focus in following Jesus. Luke 9:62 delivers a powerful metaphor to underscore the demands of discipleship, emphasizing that an unwavering focus is essential for serving God. Jesus' words challenge followers to leave behind distractions and fully dedicate themselves to His mission.

Just as a farmer plowing a field must keep his eyes fixed ahead to ensure straight rows, a disciple must avoid being distracted by past relationships, commitments, or competing priorities.

The act of "looking back" indicates divided loyalties or a reluctance to fully embrace the demands of following Jesus. Whether it involves lingering attachments to one's old life or hesitation to commit wholeheartedly, such distractions can prevent a person from fully participating in the work of God's kingdom. This verse summarizes the radical commitment required of a disciple, where every aspect of life is to be subordinated to the mission of Christ.

Modern Interpretation

In first-century Jewish culture, this statement was deeply challenging. Family and cultural obligations were paramount in their society. A total focus on Jesus was a radical undertaking. Many would have been torn between the comfort of home and the complete transformative call to discipleship.

Today's readers have other distractions but they are no less significant. Careers, personal ambitions, technology, and societal pressures can draw focus away from Christ. The metaphor of the plow resonates today as a call to examine our priorities and ensure that our commitment to Jesus is steadfast.

We should also note the phrase, "fit for service in the kingdom of God." This phrase might appear harsh or exclusionary, but it emphasizes the seriousness of discipleship. It is not about earning salvation but about the readiness to fully embrace the demands of serving God. A divided focus limits the effectiveness of a disciple.

Luke 9:62 also aligns with other New Testament teachings on discipleship:

- In Matthew 6:24, Jesus teaches that one cannot serve two masters, underscoring the necessity of undivided loyalty.

- In Luke 14:33, He emphasized that following Him requires renouncing all other attachments.

- Paul echoes this forward-focused faith in Philippians 3:13-14, where he speaks of forgetting what lies behind and pressing on toward the goal of God's calling in Christ Jesus.

These teachings collectively portray discipleship as a transformative journey that demands full attention and dedication. They challenge a casual or distracted approach to faith that doesn't account for a life centered on Christ.

When believers fully commit to being a disciple of Christ, they experience a deeper intimacy with Him and a clearer sense of purpose. A continuing focus will equip us to face challenges with perseverance and to live lives that reflect the power of the gospel. In a world filled with distractions, Jesus' words challenge us to fix our eyes on Him.

DISCUSSION QUESTIONS

8. What does it mean to "put a hand to the plow" in your spiritual journey?

9. What are some "old ways" or attachments that might tempt someone to look back? Why do you think Jesus places such urgency on not looking back when serving the Kingdom?

10. How does today's culture challenge your ability to stay focused on Jesus?

BEING FULLY COMMITTED

Revelation 3:15-16 NIV (Warning to the Church in Laodicea)
"I know your deeds, that you are neither cold nor hot. I wish you were either one or the other! So, because you are lukewarm—neither hot nor cold—I am about to spit you out of my mouth."

Revelation 3:15-16 delivers a stark and urgent message to the church in Laodicea: half-hearted faith is unacceptable in God's kingdom. Jesus rebukes spiritual complacency and calls for decisive commitment. He identifies apathy and lukewarm discipleship as serious dangers. Jesus criticizes the Laodiceans for being "lukewarm"—neither hot with zeal nor cold with conscious rejection. This state of indifference displeases Him.

The passage demands believers choose fervent dedication or deliberate rejection rather than wavering between the two. Jesus warns that He will "spit out" those who remain lukewarm, symbolizing rejection of those who fail to fully commit to Him. The core message is clear: faith must be lived out actively with passion and purpose. Half-hearted faith or a blend of nominal belief and worldly comfort simply will not work.

Modern Relevance

Laodicea was a wealthy city, known for its banking, textile production, and medical advancements, particularly its renowned eye salve. Despite its wealth the city lacked a reliable water source and had to rely on aqueducts to bring in tepid, mineral-laden water. This imagery of lukewarm water perfectly symbolized the church's spiritual state: self-sufficient, comfortable, but ineffective and thus distasteful to God.

Jesus' rebuke directly addressed the Laodicean reliance on material wealth and their apathy toward spiritual matters. They had grown complacent, valuing comfort over commitment, a condition Jesus found unacceptable.

Today's culture mirrors Laodicea's materialism and self-reliance. Many Christians face the temptation to settle into complacency, prioritizing career success, financial security, or social status over serious discipleship. This passage challenges believers to examine their faith: is it lukewarm, characterized by indifference and half-hearted effort, or is it marked by the passion of total devotion to Christ?

The harsh imagery of being spit out reflects divine judgment, emphasizing how offensive lukewarm faith is to God. It conveys that spiritual indifference cannot coexist with God's holiness or mission. Struggling with faith issues often leads to deeper faith when joined with genuine repentance. Luke-warm faith reflects a lack of effort or concern to grow spiritually.

Application

This passage invites believers to assess faith honestly: are we lukewarm; are we coasting in comfort and avoiding sacrifice; have we lost our devotion? Regular self-examination, prayer, and active participation in God's mission can help rekindle zeal.

In a world that values comfort and particularly self-sufficiency, this call challenges Christians to live counter-culturally. Total commitment involves sacrificing personal ambitions, rejecting complacency, and aligning every aspect of life with God's will. It can involve:

- **Renewal**: Regularly assessing your spiritual fervor through prayer and reflection, asking God to rekindle passion where needed.

- **Intentional Engagement**: Actively serving in your church and using your spiritual gifts for God's glory.

- **Spiritual Disciplines**: Committing to regular Bible study, prayer, and worship as a means to keep faith alive and vibrant.

- **Challenge Complacency**: Avoiding self-satisfaction in your spiritual state by setting goals for growth and seeking accountability.

- **Witness with Passion**: Sharing your faith boldly, demonstrating the joy and commitment that comes from following Jesus wholeheartedly.

DISCUSSION QUESTIONS

11. What does it mean to be "lukewarm" in faith? How can we recognize if we are in this state?

12. How does modern culture encourage believers to be lukewarm in their faith? How can believers resist?

13. How do you respond to Jesus' warning about being lukewarm? What does His offer of repentance mean to you?

14. What areas of your life (e.g., work, relationships, or habits) might reflect a lukewarm approach to faith?

OBEDIENCE

John 8:31 *"If you hold to my teaching, you are really my disciples."* NIV
1 John 2:6 *"Whoever claims to live in him must live as Jesus did."* NIV

True discipleship, as revealed in John 8:31 and 1 John 2:6, presents a profound challenge that goes far beyond mere verbal profession of faith. These passages establish a clear framework for understanding authentic Christian discipleship through two fundamental principles: (1) steadfast adherence to Jesus' teachings (modeling one's life after Christ) and (2) the active imitation of His life.

The statement "If you hold to my teaching, you are really my disciples" appears in a crucial context where Jesus was engaging with believers who were wrestling with the full implications of His message. The phrase "hold to" carries significant weight, suggesting not just intellectual agreement but a sustained commitment to living out Jesus' teachings.

The complementary passage in 1 John "Whoever claims to live in him must live as Jesus did" reinforces and expands upon Jesus' earlier teaching. This directive presents a clear standard: authentic Christian living must reflect Christ's character and conduct in practical observable ways.

In Jesus' day Jewish believers were struggling to fully embrace His teachings in their cultural and social context due to their long history of Jewish tradition and laws. Thus, early Christians faced challenges to authentic faith practices.

The phrase "hold to my teaching" should not be interpreted as legalistic rule-following, but rather as the expected response to Christ's leadership and guidance. It would involve consistent study of Scripture, practical application of biblical principles, regular self-examination, and commitment to spiritual growth.

It's important to understand this as a progressive journey rather than immediate perfection. It involves Spirit-empowered transformation and a focus on core attitudes and values as expressions in daily choices.

DISCUSSION QUESTIONS

15. What do you think "living as Jesus did" looks like in practical terms today?

16. What obstacles make it difficult to remain committed to Jesus' teachings?

SUMMARY: The Commitment of a Jesus Follower

The commitment of a Jesus follower should be total and evident for others to see. It is not based on just spoken claims or superficial religious activity, but is demonstrated through a life deeply rooted in Christ that produces <u>spiritual</u> fruit. This will glorify God because it will be reflect His character in the believer's speech, actions, and core values.

True discipleship requires abiding in Jesus (John 15:8), obeying His teachings, and producing evidence of faith through love, service, and spiritual growth. Jesus followers must not only know His words but also live them out. It is the hallmark of genuine faith, distinguishing authentic followers from those who only appear religious (Matthew 7:20-21).

We have examined a number of passages that collectively paint a vivid picture of the depth and breadth of the commitment desired from a follower of Jesus. These teachings challenge us to embody a radical and all-encompassing dedication to Christ.

We have observed the following key themes of a life committed to Christ:

- Supreme loyalty to Christ.
- Self-denial and cross-bearing.
- Undivided focus.
- Authentic obedience.
- Bearing fruit for God's glory.
- Not loving the world.

The commitment of a Jesus follower is radical, countercultural, and deeply transformative. It is marked by serious commitment where faith is a priority. Following Jesus is a life of faithfulness and love reflecting true discipleship. Genuine commitment is consistent with God's Word and is lived out in actions, not merely words.

Wisdom to Action
Challenge

Reflect on your daily choices and actions. What is one concrete step you can take today to align your life more closely with God's will and bring Him pleasure?

Lesson 3
Choose Enduring Faith

" How narrow is the gate and difficult the road that leads to life, and few find it."
Matthew 7:14 HCSB

An enduring faith requires one to persevere through challenges and difficulties that might endanger one's faith. We will not include the topic of perseverance or standing firm in this lesson as we cover these subjects in Lesson #10. Rather in this lesson we will focus on other characteristics of our faith that help and encourage us to endure. We will end the lesson by looking at Matthew 7:13-14 that says believers must enter through the *narrow* gate.

LIVING BY FAITH

Let's first examine the important passages in the New Testament that speak to living our lives *by faith*.

Galatians 2:20 *I have been crucified with Christ and I no longer live, but Christ lives in me. The life I now live in the body, I live by faith in the Son of God, who loved me and gave himself for me.* NIV

> **Key Point:** A disciple's life is fully surrendered to Christ's control.

2 Timothy 4:7-8 *I have fought the good fight, I have finished the race, I have kept the faith. Now there is in store for me the* crown of righteousness, which the Lord, the righteous Judge, will award to me on that day—and not only to me, but also to all who have longed for his appearing. NIV

>**Key Point:** Perseverance in faith is essential to receiving eternal rewards.

2 Corinthians 1:23-24 But I call God to witness against me—it was to spare you that I refrained from coming again to Corinth. 24 Not that we lord it over your faith, but we work with you for your joy, for you stand firm in your faith. ESV

>**Key Point:** We are to stand firm in our faith.

Hebrews 10:38 But my righteous one shall live by faith, and if he shrinks back, my soul has no pleasure in him. ESV

2 Corinthians 5:7 for we walk by faith, not by sight. ESV

>**Key Point:** We are to walk in obedience, trusting God beyond visible circumstances in His promises and character. We should take action based on faith, not doubt or fear: we are to live by faith, not sight.

FAITH DESCRIBED

Hebrews 11:1-7 Now faith is the assurance of things hoped for, the conviction of things not seen. 2 For by it the people of old received their commendation. 3 By faith we understand that the universe was created by the word of God, so that what is seen was not made out of things that are visible. 4 By faith Abel offered to God a more acceptable sacrifice than Cain, through which he was commended as righteous, God commending him by accepting his gifts. And through his faith, though he died, he still speaks. 5 By faith Enoch was taken up so that he should not see death, and he was not found, because God had taken him. Now before he was taken he was commended as having pleased God. 6 And without faith it is impossible to please him, for *whoever would draw near to God must believe that he exists and that he rewards those who seek him.* ESV

This passage introduces faith as the foundation of a believer's relationship with God and as the guiding principle for a life that *pleases* Him. It emphasizes that enduring faith involves trust in His promises, even when they are unseen. It translates into actions that align with His will. Enduring faith is not passive belief but an active trust in God that shapes one's actions and outlook. It is a faith that trusts God even when His actions are invisible or delayed.

Faith is described above as *"the assurance of things hoped for, the conviction of things not seen."* Enduring faith means confidently trusting in the reality of His unseen work, regardless of our immediate circumstances. The examples in the passage demonstrate that faith pleases God and is the foundation for a life lived in alignment with His purposes.

The author of Hebrews describes several examples of faith in action (verses 4-7):

> ABEL: Offered a better sacrifice than Cain, showing that faith leads to worship and giving that pleases God.

> ENOCH: Walked faithfully with God and was taken up to Him without death, illustrating that faith fosters an intimate relationship with God.

> NOAH: Obeyed God's warning about unseen events and built the ark, demonstrating that faith involves obedience and trust in God's guidance, even when it defies human understanding.

Both Abel and Noah are commended as righteous because of their faith. Righteousness is not earned but credited through a faith-filled relationship with God. Enduring faith means we trust beyond what is visible. Just as Noah trusted God's warning about unseen dangers, believers today are called to trust in

God's promises about salvation, eternity, purpose, and protection.

Enduring faith compels us to live in obedience and alignment with God's will. Like Enoch, enduring faith fosters a deep personal walk with God, rooted in continuing worship and relationship. Abel's faith-filled offering challenges believers to give generously, reflecting trust in God as the provider.

GENUINE FAITH

1 Peter 1:3-7 *Blessed be the God and Father of our Lord Jesus Christ! According to his great mercy, he has caused us to be born again to a living hope through the resurrection of Jesus Christ from the dead, 4 to an inheritance that is imperishable, undefiled, and unfading, kept in heaven for you, 5 who by God's power are being guarded through faith for a salvation ready to be revealed in the last time. 6 In this you rejoice, though now for a little while, if necessary, you have been grieved by various trials, 7 so that the tested genuineness of your faith—more precious than gold that perishes though it is tested by fire—may be found to result in praise and glory and honor at the revelation of Jesus Christ.* ESV

We should desire a strong and genuine faith in following Jesus. We may need courage to boldly step out in faith, even beyond our comfort zones. We should trust Jesus completely in all things with a strong unbreakable faith that never wavers. Our faith should help us remain steadfast when difficulties arise. Our response to difficulties should not be depression and loss of hope. We should rejoice in trials that refine our faith (often easier said than done). Perseverance will build spiritual maturity and trust in God's sovereignty. Our faith can thrive when it is anchored in God's promises and not life's circumstances.

Our most obvious response should be to pray for strength and wisdom when facing challenges. We can also memorize the promises of Scripture to combat doubt and discouragement. Remember we are told that if we come near to God He will come near to us (James 4:8). We should trust Him in all circumstances, thus we can pray for:

- a strong unbreakable faith that never wavers,
- a faith that is a pleasing sacrifice,
- an enduring faith resulting from righteous living, and
- a faith that will be proven genuine (1 Peter 1:3-7).

2 Timothy 3:10-11 *You, however, have followed my teaching, my conduct, my aim in life, my faith, my patience, my love, my steadfastness, 11 my persecutions and sufferings that happened to me at Antioch, at Iconium, and at Lystra—which persecutions I endured; yet from them all the Lord rescued me.* ESV

Paul persevered in suffering! We may need to do the same. We are not promised an easy life in this fallen world. There will undoubtedly be problems and even suffering. Paul told us how the Lord rescued him from his persecutions and sufferings.

ENTER THROUGH THE NARROW GATE

Matthew 7:13-14 *Enter through the narrow gate. For the gate is wide and the road is broad that leads to destruction, and there are many who go through it. 14 How narrow is the gate and difficult the road that leads to life, and few find it.* HCSB

Jesus used the imagery of two gates and two roads to emphasize the distinct paths available to humanity. The narrow path represents the way of discipleship and commitment to Jesus/God, while the wide road signifies the way of ease, conformity, and destruction.

Key Points

The Narrow Gate: Access requires intentionality, self-denial, and alignment with God's will. It symbolizes the disciplined faith of following Jesus, characterized by obedience and sacrifice, when necessary. True discipleship is demanding! Many will reject this path and refuse the offer of life.

The Broad Road: This path is easy and accommodating but ultimately leads to destruction and disappointment. It represents living without regard to God's standards or commands. The road may be crowded.

Core Message

This passage underscores the exclusivity and difficulty of following Jesus. The path to eternal life requires a deliberate choice, marked by total commitment and perseverance. This passage aligns with other New Testament Scriptures that stress the cost of discipleship (e.g., Luke 9:23-24; John 14:6) and the necessity of entering through Jesus, who is the only "gate" to salvation (John 10:9).

It also aligns with Luke 14:25-33, which calls for wholehearted devotion to Jesus. Jesus' statement in John 14:6, emphasizing that Jesus alone is the way to eternal life, clearly describes the exclusive nature of Christian discipleship.

The phrases "narrow gate" and "broad road" may seem harsh in modern contexts but must be understood as metaphors for the realities of discipleship. The narrow gate represents a life surrendered to God's will pursuant to the teachings of Christ, while the broad road reflects the dangers of self-centered living.

Jesus' audience lived in a pluralistic and religiously diverse culture surrounded by both Roman paganism and Jewish legalism. The imagery of gates and roads would resonate with readers as visual markers of decision-making, emphasizing the importance of choosing God's way over cultural or religious norms.

It is worth noting that there are several important theological themes in play in this passage. We have already alluded to the exclusive nature of salvation which is found only through Jesus (John 14:6). Following Jesus requires sacrifice, discipline, and perseverance (Luke 9:23-24). There is a cost for being a Jesus follower. The danger is described by the reference to a broad road which leads to destruction. This highlights the consequences of rejecting God's way (Romans 6:23). Finally the passage warns that true discipleship will not be embraced by the majority (Matthew 22:14).

SUMMARY: Narrow vs. Wide

If we were to compare and contrast the narrow path versus the wide road:

Narrow	vs	*Wide/broad*
1. Hardship/difficult	vs	Easy

There is never an easy way to greatness. Greatness is always the product of toil. Wickedness and apathy are easy choices

2. Long	vs	Short way

Greatness is nearly always the result of long labor and constant attention to detail. We are constantly faced with choosing the short or long way.

3. Disciplined lifestyle	vs	Unrestricted life

Nothing is achieved without discipline! Many have been ruined because they refused or abandoned discipline.

4. Thoughtful	vs	Thoughtless

Everything in world has two looks: how it appears now and what it will be in the future. We must look at things in the light of eternity.

5. Fewer people	vs	Many people
6. High standard of conduct	vs.	More popular; Self determined standards

7. Requires a decision	vs	Requires no decisions
8. Appears less attractive	vs	No or less resistance
9. Promise of eternal life	vs	No promise given

PERSONAL CHALLENGE

If we were experiencing a real spiritual challenge we should want to evaluate our commitments. We might regularly assess whether our choices aligned with God's will or if they reflected worldly priorities. We would want to commit to practices like prayer, Bible study, and serving others as part of walking the narrow path. We would try to stand firm in faith against the culture.

To have success we need to rely on God's strength. We recognize that perseverance on the narrow path comes from dependence on God's grace and strength, not on our own efforts.

The obvious response to life's challenges is to spend time in prayer, asking God to reveal areas of your life that need alignment with His will. You might want to make one intentional decision each week that reflects the values of the narrow way (e.g., forgiving someone, serving sacrificially, etc.). We suggest you join a small group or have an accountability partner in order to encourage you to stay committed to the path of discipleship.

Lastly, share your faith with someone who may be walking on the broad road. They need to hear from you!

DISCUSSION AND THOUGHT QUESTIONS

1. In this lesson we are talking about making important life decisions. What happens if we avoid or delay the important issues?

2. Some choices don't really have much impact on life, but many do.

   a. What are the kind of <u>secular</u> choices that really matter?

   b. What are the kind of <u>spiritual</u> choices that really matter?

3. Why is it important to consider the destination when embarking on a trip or beginning some life journey?

4. How would you relate the message of the narrow gate in Matthew 7:13-14 to what Jesus had been preaching previously in His Sermon on the Mount (Matthew 5-6)?

5. If you don't choose the narrow gate, what road have you chosen?

6. How would <u>you</u> describe the "Narrow Road"?

7. Given there is a "narrow" gate, what does that mean or imply for gaining entrance?

8. What makes the wide road tempting?

9. Why would <u>you</u> personally consider the narrow road difficult?

10. Why do you think Jesus described the preferred road or gate as *narrow*?

11. Why do you think many say that Christianity will never be a majority movement?

12. Why would someone intentionally choose the wide road?

13. How does Matthew 7:21 address the narrow versus wide question? Matthew 7:21-22 "Not everyone who says to me, 'Lord, Lord,' will enter the kingdom of heaven, but only he who does the will of my Father who is in heaven." NIV

14. How would you personally reconcile the challenges of the narrow way with the life Jesus promises to His followers?

Wisdom to Action
Challenge

In what ways can you actively nurture your relationship with Christ this week? Consider how you can apply a specific teaching from God's Word to transform an aspect of your lifestyle or service to others.

Lesson 4
Lordship, Surrender, and Submission

"And God placed all things under his feet and appointed him to be head over everything for the church, which is his body, the fullness of him who fills everything in every way."
Ephesians 1:22-23 (NIV)

LORDSHIP

Lordship can be simply defined as accepting the sovereignty of God. If we truly believe that there is a God and that He is the God of Abraham, Isaac, and Jacob, then the concept of His sovereignty is much easier to understand and accept. If our view of God is something less than His being the Creator, Provider, Healer, and Sustainer of life then it may be challenging to unconditionally submit or surrender to His authority.

For those who know Jesus as Savior and Lord, biblical Lordship can be described as:

- God having power and authority over a follower.
- A repentant sinner *submitting* to the will of God.
- The state of being obedient.
- The act of accepting Jesus as Lord and master of life.
- Being submissive, humble, or compliant to Jesus.
- Yielding power and control to the Spirit of God (surrender).

The Lordship of Christ refers to the authority and supreme rule of Jesus over all creation, as well as His rightful place as Lord over the lives of those who believe in Him. This entails recognizing and submitting to Jesus not only as Savior but also as the absolute Master and King in all areas of life: He is Lord!

But, the Lordship is voluntary! A Jesus follower must accept and agree that Jesus is God and deserves his submission. He is the sovereign Lord and their personal Savior/Redeemer. The committed disciple accepts the role of a "slave," being completely surrendered to God ruling in their life.[1]

Christ's Authority

Jesus claims the role of universal Lord over His people. He is proclaimed as Lord over all creation because He is both Creator and Sustainer. Colossians 1:16 confirms His authority and rule: *"For by Him all things were created, in heaven and on earth, visible and invisible, whether thrones or dominions or rulers or authorities—all things were created through Him and for Him."* ESV

After His resurrection, Jesus was exalted to the highest place of authority. Philippians 2:9-10 says, *"Therefore God has highly exalted Him and bestowed on Him the name that is above every name, so that at the name of Jesus every knee should bow."* ESV Jesus is described fully by Paul in his letter to the Colossians:

> **Colossians 1:15-20** *He is the image of the invisible God, the firstborn of all creation. 16 For by him all things were created, in heaven and on earth, visible and invisible, whether thrones or dominions or rulers or authorities—all things were created through him and for him. 17 And he is before all things, and in him all things hold together. 18 And he is the head of the body, the church. He is the beginning, the firstborn from the dead, that in everything he might be preeminent. 19 For in him all the fullness of God was pleased to dwell, 20 and through him to reconcile to himself all things, whether on earth or in heaven, making peace by the blood of his cross.* ESV

In this passage Jesus' authority as the "head of the body, the church" is confirmed. Not only is He the creator and sustainer of all things but He rules as head of the church and is described as the One who brings peace.

JESUS IS LORD

Whenever worshiping Christians repeat the Church's earliest confession of faith, "Jesus is Lord," they are confirming their relationship to the Divine. He is the One in Colossians 1:18 who is preeminent, meaning having the supreme rank in His relationship to the church. Thus, He is the Lord of our lives:

HE IS THE CHRIST: The Christ (Messiah) of our faith is none other than the Jesus of history (Acts 2:34-36).

HE IS GOD: Being Lord acknowledges the deity of Christ (John 20:28; Philippians 2:6, 9-11).

HE IS SUPREME: He is sovereign which proclaims His personal right to absolute supremacy in the universe, the Church, and our individual lives (Acts 10:36; Romans 10:12; 14:8; 1 Corinthians 8:6; James 4:15).

HE IS SAVIOR: The Lord is our Redeemer which affirms the triumph of Christ over death and hostile cosmic powers when God raised Him from the dead (Romans 10:9; 14:9; Ephesians 1:20-22; Colossians 2:10, 15).

HE IS ALIVE: He is the Christian's hope of resurrection (1 Corinthians 6:14; 2 Corinthians 4:14).

HE IS THE GOSPEL: His message is life (Romans 10:8; 2 Corinthians 4:5).

HE IS THE RIGHTEOUS JUDGE: Everyone is accountable to the Lord, the Righteous Judge (1 Corinthians 4:5; 2 Timothy 4:1, 8).

HE SENT THE SPIRIT: Our confession is a personal and public declaration of faith (Romans 10:9), which testifies to our being led by the Holy Spirit (1 Corinthians 12:3).

HE IS CREATOR: His rule repudiates the former allegiance to any pagan gods and reaffirms our loyalty to the one Lord through whom and in whom we existed (1 Timothy 6:15).[2]

Thus, a Christian can state his desire or intent regarding his relationship with Christ as follows:

- I want to live confidently under the <u>Lordship</u> of Christ.
- I want to be a <u>slave</u> of Christ and the Gospel of Truth.
- I want to live in <u>submission</u> to Christ.
- I want to be <u>surrendered</u> to Christ in all aspects of my life.

LORDSHIP OVER ALL ASPECTS OF LIFE

Your involvement in worship, Bible study, and prayer will reflect your attitude toward Christ's position as Lord of your life. But His impact on a true Jesus follower goes beyond the normal activities of a disciple. The following describes other aspects of life that will involve making Jesus Lord of your life.

1. OBEDIENCE: Recognizing Christ as Lord means living in obedience to His teachings. Luke 6:46 says, *"Why do you call me 'Lord, Lord,' and not do what I tell you?"* (ESV)

2. DEVOTION: It requires surrendering every part of life—thoughts, actions, desires, and relationships—to His control: *"And He died for all, that those who live might no longer live for themselves but for Him who for their sake died and was raised"* (2 Corinthians 5:15 ESV).

3. DAILY LIVING: Decisions, behaviors, and priorities are guided by His will: *"Whatever you do, in word or deed, do everything in the name of the Lord Jesus"* (Colossians 3:17 ESV).

4. RELATIONSHIPS: Serving others, forgiving, and loving reflect His lordship: *"For we do not live to ourselves, and we do not die*

to ourselves. If we live, we live to the Lord, and if we die, we die to the Lord" (Romans 14:7-8 ESV).

5. HIS PROVISION: We live life trusting and depending on God for all of our needs. We trust in God's timing, provision and care: "*And my God will supply every need of yours according to his riches in glory in Christ Jesus.*" (Philippians 4:19 ESV)

6. KINGDOM OF GOD: While Christ may be Lord, His ultimate reign won't be fully realized until He returns to establish His eternal kingdom: "*Then comes the end, when He delivers the kingdom to God the Father after destroying every rule and every authority and power.*" (1 Corinthians 15:24 ESV)

7. PRIORITY: Seek first the kingdom of God and His righteousness. Jesus is Lord over all aspects of life:

> **Matthew 6:33** *But seek first the kingdom of God and his righteousness, and all these things will be added to you.* ESV
> **Philippians 4:19-20** *And my God will supply every need of yours according to his riches in glory in Christ Jesus. 20 To our God and Father be glory forever and ever. Amen.* ESV

The Jesus follower prioritizes God's kingdom and His will because he aligns his life goals and actions with God's purposes. Building God's kingdom and adhering to His purposes are more important than personal gain or worldly pursuits. It means aligning one's life with God's will and trusting in His provision.

8. EXCLUSIVE: Following Jesus means complete dedication to His lordship. It means denying self and taking up your cross daily (see Lesson #5): Matthew 16:24-25 *Then Jesus told his disciples, "If anyone would come after me, let him deny himself and take up his cross and follow me. 25 For whoever would save his life will lose it, but whoever loses his life for my sake will find it."* ESV

9. SERVICE: Actively serve under Christ. Proverbs 3:5-6 "*Trust in the Lord with all your heart, and do not lean on your own understanding. 6 In all your ways acknowledge him, and he will make straight your paths.*" ESV

Practical Implications

Believers trust in Christ's authority, even in trials and suffering, knowing He is the sovereign God of all creation. Living under Christ's Lordship means growing in love and obedience with His will, and trying to eliminate sin from daily life.

The Lordship of Christ is not merely a doctrinal statement but a call to a life of complete allegiance, worship, and service to Him as the sovereign Ruler and King.

Jesus' dual roles of Savior and Lord are generally inseparable. A genuine faith in Jesus as Savior includes submitting to Him as Lord: Romans 10:9 says, "*If you confess with your mouth that Jesus is Lord and believe in your heart that God raised Him from the dead, you will be saved."* ESV

SUBMISSION/SURRENDER TO CHRIST

The Bible closely intertwines the concepts of submission and surrender to Christ, but there are some subtle distinctions between the two, particularly in their emphasis and application. The Bible presents submission and surrender as complementary facets of a disciple's relationship with Christ. Both involve yielding to His Lordship, but they emphasize different dimensions: submission is a daily practice of obedience and alignment, and surrender is a complete act of trust and relinquishment. Together, they embody the essence of what it means to follow Jesus wholeheartedly.

Submission: Voluntary Alignment

Submission refers to a willful acknowledgment of and alignment under the authority and rule of Christ. It implies a conscious decision to obey God, accept His leadership, and yield to His will in all aspects of life. There are three important aspects to submission:

- **Obedience**: Following God's commandments and teachings (James 4:7).

- **Humility**: Recognizing God's sovereignty and humbling oneself before Him (1 Peter 5:6).

- **Ongoing Submission**: This involves a continual choice to align with God's will daily.

For example we see Jesus in the Garden of Gethsemane saying: "Not my will, but Yours be done" (Luke 22:42). And in Ephesians 5:21 believers are submitting to one another out of reverence for Christ.

Biblical Basis for Submission

- **Acknowledging Christ's Lordship**:
  "Submit yourselves therefore to God. Resist the devil, and he will flee from you" (James 4:7 ESV).
  Submission to God inherently includes submission to Christ as Lord, as He has the ultimate authority given by the Father (Matthew 28:18).

- **Obedience as a Form of Submission**:
  "If you love me, you will keep my commandments" (John 14:15 ESV).
  Obeying Christ's teachings is a demonstration of submitting to His authority in love and devotion.

- **Relational Submission**:
  "And be subject to one another out of reverence for Christ" (Ephesians 5:21 ESV).
  Believers submit to one another in relationships, reflecting their greater submission to Christ.

Surrender: Total Yielding

Surrender emphasizes the act of giving up personal control and agendas to trust God completely. It involves handing over every aspect of life to Christ—heart, mind, soul, and body—trusting

His plan above one's own desires or understanding. Again there are three important aspects to observe:

- **Trust**: Fully relying on God's sovereignty and goodness (Proverbs 3:5-6).

- **Finality**: Surrender often carries a connotation of relinquishment that is comprehensive and irrevocable.

- **Inner Transformation**: Surrender leads to profound heart change as we let God shape and direct our lives.

We see an example of this in Paul's declaration: *"I have been crucified with Christ and I no longer live, but Christ lives in me"* (Galatians 2:20 NIV). It is also the breaking point for the rich young ruler in Mark 10:21-22.

Biblical Basis for Surrender

Surrender to Christ may go a step further than submission by emphasizing the complete relinquishment of self-will and control, handing over everything to Christ in trust and faith.

- **Dying to Self**:
  "If anyone would come after me, let him deny himself and take up his cross daily and follow me" (Luke 9:23 ESV). True surrender means forsaking personal ambitions and following Christ's leading.

- **Living for Christ**:
  "I have been crucified with Christ. It is no longer I who live, but Christ who lives in me" (Galatians 2:20 ESV). Surrender involves yielding one's entire life so that Christ may reign within.

Submission focuses on accepting and obeying Christ's authority. It's an act of aligning oneself under His leadership. *Surrender* goes somewhat deeper, involving a relinquishment of self in trust and dependency on Christ's grace and sovereignty.

Summary

While the two concepts overlap, submission is often associated with obedience and positioning oneself under Christ's authority, while surrender highlights a deeper relinquishment of self and trust in God's sovereignty. Submission focuses on the act of yielding to God's will in daily decisions. Surrender involves the state of being fully yielded, trusting God with one's entire life and future.

In practice, both are essential for a disciple of Christ. Submission often flows from a heart that has first surrendered to Christ. Surrender lays the foundation for a life of ongoing submission, as seen in Romans 12:1: *"Present your bodies as a living sacrifice, holy and acceptable to God, which is your spiritual worship."* ESV

Submitting or surrendering to Christ as Savior and Lord means we are living in a state of obedience to His will. We accept His authority over our lives and allow His rule. He sits on the throne of our heart. We are living in the light of Micah 6:8 which tells us to "walk humbly with our God."

While the exact phrases "submission to Christ" or "surrender to Christ" are not explicitly found in Scripture, the principles are clearly taught. Believers are called to submit to Christ's authority in obedience and to surrender their lives to Him in trust, love, and devotion. Both submission and surrender are essential aspects of living as a true follower of Jesus.

SUBMITTING TO ONE ANOTHER – Marriage

Submit to one another out of reverence for Christ. 22 Wives, submit to your husbands as to the Lord. . . . 24 Now as the church submits to Christ, so also wives should submit to their husbands in everything. Husbands, love your wives, just as Christ loved the church and gave himself up for her 26 to make her holy, cleansing her by the washing with water through the word, 27 and to present her to himself as a radiant church, without stain or wrinkle or any other blemish, but holy and blameless. 28

In this same way, husbands ought to love their wives as their own bodies. He who loves his wife loves himself. . . . 33 However, each one of you also must love his wife as he loves himself, and the wife must respect her husband.
(Ephesians 5:21-22, 24-28, 33 NIV)

Submitting means we yield ourselves to the authority or will of another. Biblically this means vowing to *submit* to the will of God with respect to relationships and permit oneself to be subjected to something or someone else. It can mean one will defer to or consent to abide by the opinion or authority of another. Thus submitting includes:

- Being obedient or compliant to another.
- Accepting the authority/control of another.
- Being subject to another.
- Yielding control of oneself to another.
- Yielding power, control, or possession to another.

This passage from Ephesians offers guidance on the roles and responsibilities within a Christian marriage and family, emphasizing <u>mutual</u> submission and sacrificial love.

In the context of marriage, it directs wives to "submit yourselves to your own husbands as you do to the Lord" (v. 22) highlighting a respectful and supportive partnership. Husbands are instructed to love their wives just as Christ loved the church (v. 25). This sacrificial love involves cherishing, nurturing, and prioritizing the well-being of their wives. The passage further indicates that husbands should love their wives as their own bodies, emphasizing care and unity (v. 28).

Ephesians 5:33 summarizes the relationship dynamics: "Each one of you also must love his wife as he loves himself, and the wife must respect her husband." This mutual respect and love create a harmonious and godly relationship, reflecting the love Christ has for the church. This passage calls for a balanced partnership where both husband and wife love and respect each other, creating a strong foundation for a Christian family.

MEDITATION QUESTIONS

Consider the following questions and meditate on your answers.

- Do I consider Jesus the Lord of my life?
- Is Jesus on the throne of my life?
- Can I truly say that Jesus is the master and authority in my life?
- Is Jesus really in control, or just when I allow Him at my convenience?
- Who is really in charge/control of my life?

DISCUSSION AND THOUGHT QUESTIONS

1. What does the "Lordship of Christ" mean to you?

2. Do you take His Lordship seriously? Would others recognize His Lordship in your life?

3. When is the last time you rejected His Lordship? Alternatively, "Have you ever really accepted His Lordship?" How does your life reflect His Lordship?

4. What would you tell a new believer it means to live in submission to Christ?

5. What are your biggest hurdles? Is submission/surrender a mental, physical, emotional, or spiritual hurdle for you? Why?

6. Why do people generally have difficulty with surrender/submission?

7. Is submission really that important? How important or unimportant is this subject in your personal faith walk?

8. Do <u>you</u> think you can have a real relationship with Christ without true submission? Explain.

9. How could you illustrate the concept of surrender and submission in a real life example or illustration?

10. Do you have a personal story you could share about the concept of surrender/submission?

11. What must you <u>personally</u> <u>do</u> or <u>not do</u> to truly conform to the need to surrender/submit?

DO:

NOT DO:

UNIQUE/SPECIAL CIRCUMSTANCES:

12. What is the result or benefit of surrender/submission?

13. With regard to the Challenges in the Lesson above:

13a. Are there important questions missing from the list above? What would you add?

13b. What do you believe is the most critical question in the list? Why?

14. What are you going to do about this challenge in your life? What are your next steps?

Wisdom to Action
Challenge

Examine your priorities this week. What one thing can you adjust to demonstrate that Christ truly comes first in your life? How will this change reflect your devotion to Him?

Lesson 5
Take Up Your CROSS

"If anyone would come after me, let him deny himself and take up his cross and follow me. For whoever would save his life will lose it, but whoever loses his life for my sake will find it. For what will it profit a man if he gains the whole world and forfeits his life?"
Matthew 16:24-26 (ESV)

DENY YOURSELF – TAKE UP YOUR CROSS

Following Jesus often means sacrificing personal comfort, enduring hardship, and living selflessly. Taking up your cross reflects a readiness to embrace sacrifice, if necessary. It means being willing to endure hardship. A committed Jesus follower will be willing to deny himself as needed.

Denying yourself and taking up your cross may require loving others sacrificially. These others could be family, friends, or just casual acquaintances. We treat others as we would want to be treated. The passage in Matthew 16 is a powerful call to discipleship and describes the nature and commitment required of a truly committed Jesus follower. Jesus says:

- **Deny yourself**: Followers must relinquish self-centeredness, personal ambitions, and desires that conflict with God's will.

- **Take up your cross**: This metaphor implies a willingness to embrace suffering or sacrifice for the sake of Christ. In the Roman world, carrying a cross was a symbol of submission to authority and an acknowledgment of impending execution.

- ***Follow me***: Discipleship is an active and ongoing process. It requires a continual commitment to walking in Jesus' footsteps and emulating His life and teachings.

In Matthew 16:25 Jesus introduces a paradox for living as a Jesus follower. He says that those who seek to preserve their lives through focus on self will lose them. The passage takes on an eternal perspective by indicating the value of the faithful follower surpasses worldly gain, and sacrificing one's self for earthly benefits results in eternal loss.

Core Message

The central message is about the cost and nature of true discipleship. Similar demands for discipleship are echoed by Paul in Galatians 2:20: *"I have been crucified with Christ. It is no longer I who live, but Christ who lives in me."* (ESV) In contrast, while the demands are rigorous, they align with Jesus' promise of abundant life in John 10:10. This balance emphasizes that true life and joy come from a surrendered life.

Understanding "take up your cross" in this context is very important. It does not mean bearing general hardships (e.g. a difficult job), but willingly facing persecution, suffering, and even death as a result of one's *allegiance* to Christ.

We should also observe several theological themes that occur in this passage.

- **Self-denial and sacrifice**: The passage underscores the essence of Christian commitment—dying to self to live for Christ (Romans 12:1-2).

- **Eternal perspective**: It highlights the priceless value of the soul and the ultimate futility of worldly pursuits apart from God (1 John 2:15-17).

- **Christ-centered living**: The call to follow Jesus establishes Him as both the model and the goal of discipleship.

Application

This passage challenges Jesus followers to live boldly:

- **Daily surrender**: Start each day with a prayer of self-denial, asking God to align your will with His.

- **Identifying your "cross:"** Recognize specific ways you are called to sacrifice for Christ—whether in relationships, career choices, or standing up for truth.

- **Living counter-culturally**: Be willing to stand up for your values, even if it will bring criticism or discomfort.

- **Seeking community support**: Join a small group for accountability and encouragement in living out the call to discipleship.

HOLD ONTO THE VINE

John 15:1-8 *I am the true vine, and my Father is the vinedresser. 2 Every branch of mine that does not bear fruit he takes away, and every branch that does bear fruit he prunes, that it may bear more fruit. 3 Already you are clean because of the word that I have spoken to you. 4 Abide in me, and I in you. As the branch cannot bear fruit by itself, unless it abides in the vine, neither can you, unless you abide in me. 5 I am the vine; you are the branches. Whoever abides in me and I in him, he it is that bears much fruit, for apart from me you can do nothing. 6 If anyone does not abide in me he is thrown away like a branch and withers; and the branches are gathered, thrown into the fire, and burned. 7 If you abide in me, and my words abide in you, ask whatever you wish, and it will be done for you. 8 By this my Father is glorified, that you bear much fruit and so prove to be my disciples.* ESV

This passage uses the metaphor of the vine and branches to describe the ideal relationship between Jesus and His followers, emphasizing their dependence on Him for spiritual power and fruitfulness. It teaches five important concepts:

1. **Jesus is the True Vine**: Jesus is the source of spiritual life, and believers must remain connected to Him to thrive.

2. **The Father is the Gardener**: God the Father nurtures the vine by pruning branches to maximize fruitfulness and removing those that bear no fruit.

3. **We are to abide in Christ**: The term "abide" (or "remain") signifies an ongoing, close relationship with Jesus, marked by trust, obedience, and intimacy.

4. **We are to bear fruit**: Fruitfulness is the evidence of abiding in Christ and includes qualities such as love, righteousness, and good works (Galatians 5:22-23).

5. **Apart From Christ, there is little value**: Jesus emphasizes that apart from Him, believers can do nothing of eternal value.

The core message is that Jesus follower must remain in a close dependent relationship with Christ in order to bear spiritual fruit and fulfill their purpose in the church. That close relationship is often referred to as abiding.

Unlike the active metaphor of taking up the cross, abiding focuses on maintaining a relationship with Christ that empowers action and fruitfulness. This describes an ongoing and life-sustaining connection with Christ. Abiding means to stay connected or continue in a close or intimate relationship with Jesus, much like a branch remains attached to the vine to receive life and nourishment. It implies a continuous active fellowship with Christ and reliance on Him for spiritual growth, strength, and fruitfulness.

Key Elements of Abiding:

Union with Christ: Abiding begins with being "grafted" into Christ, the True Vine (John 15:1). This union begins when a person puts his faith in Jesus for salvation (John 3:16; Ephesians 2:8-9).

Dependence on Christ: Just as a branch depends on the vine for sustenance, disciples must rely on Jesus for their spiritual strength and guidance. Jesus says, "*Apart from me you can do nothing*" (John 15:5), emphasizing our total dependence on Him.

Obedience to His Word: Abiding involves obeying Christ's teachings and letting His words dwell richly within us (John 15:7; Colossians 3:16). Obedience is the resulting tangible expression of our love for Him (John 14:15).

Bearing Fruit: The evidence of abiding is the fruit: characteristics such as love, joy, peace, patience, and other fruit of the Spirit (Galatians 5:22-23), as well as actions that glorify God and advance His kingdom (John 15:8). A branch that does not bear fruit will be pruned or rehabilitated to produce results that last (John 15:2, 6).

Prayerful Fellowship: Abiding includes a fervent prayer life, where believers communicate with God and align their will with His. Jesus says, "*If you remain in me and my words remain in you, ask whatever you wish, and it will be done for you*" (John 15:7).

To abide in Christ is to live in constant awareness of His presence, drawing on His strength, and submitting to His will in every area of life. It is not a passive existence but an active and ongoing commitment to stay connected to Him.

When believers abide in Christ, they experience His vitality which flows through them like sap through a branch, nourishing their souls. Their lives will reflect the character of Christ and will impact others for His glory (John 15:8). Abiding leads to fullness of joy (John 15:11) and confidence. Thus, abiding is the essence of discipleship. It is both a responsibility and a privilege that leads to a transformed life, marked by spiritual fruit and intimate fellowship.

In verse 2 John speaks of pruning. This implies God's discipline and refinement in a believer's life in order to promote growth. It may involve trials or challenges designed to remove hindrances to spiritual fruitfulness. In verse 5 Jesus says, "*Apart from me, you can do nothing.*" This does not mean believers are incapable of any action but emphasizes that abundant spiritual fruit with _eternal_ significance is impossible without Christ.

The imagery of the vine would have been familiar to Jesus' audience because vineyards were a common part of agricultural life in those days. In the Old Testament Israel is often depicted as a vine (Isaiah 5:1-7) making Jesus' claim as the "true vine" a significant theological statement.

Personal Application

The call to abide means we cultivate spiritual disciplines such as prayer, meditation, and worship in order to be connected to Christ. We may also experience His pruning in our lives. We should maximize the opportunities that God places in our path in order to grow in understanding and wisdom. We should intentionally align our actions with God's will. We must reject the evil aspects of earthly life and embrace God's strength in all we do in order to reflect His character to the world.

Taking up one's cross emphasizes self-denial and sacrifice, while abiding in Christ focuses on relationship and dependence. Both require surrender but on different aspects of discipleship. Love is the fruit of abiding in Christ, as our ability to love comes from abiding in Him. Abiding in Christ provides the spiritual strength necessary to take up our cross, deny self, and count the cost. Without this connection the sacrifices of discipleship become unsustainable.

By tying these concepts together, the commitment of a Jesus follower emerges as both relational (abiding in Christ) and sacrificial (taking up the cross). Both aspects are inseparable as the relational dependence on Christ empowers the sacrificial lifestyle required of His disciples.

DISCUSSION AND THOUGHT QUESTIONS

1. What do <u>you</u> think it means to "deny yourself"?

2. What did Jesus mean by "take up your cross"? How is this concept relevant today?

3. Why does Jesus contrast losing and saving one's life? How do you interpret this paradox?

4. What does "gaining the whole world but forfeiting the soul" look like in today's culture?

5. How can we *practically* follow Jesus in a world that often opposes His teachings?

6. What motivates <u>you</u> to embrace the cost of discipleship?

7. What practical steps can a person take to "renounce all they have" in today's culture?

8. Why does Jesus ask for such a high level of commitment? How does this compare to other commitments in life?

9. What are some ways you can support others in their discipleship journey?

10. How would you explain what it means to "abide" in Christ, and how does it affect your daily life?

11. What are some personal challenges you might experience given the passages in this lesson? For example: (a) denying yourself, (b) sacrificing for others, (c) surrender/submission, (d) abiding, etc.

12. What are some "pruning" experiences you have faced, and how did they contribute to your growth?

13. How does this passage challenge self-reliance in your spiritual walk?

14. Why do you think Jesus emphasizes that "apart from me, you can do nothing"?

Wisdom to Action
Challenge

What personal desire or comfort are you holding onto that may be hindering your full commitment to Christ? How can you "take up your cross" in this area and follow Jesus more closely?

Exhibit
Biblical heroes who were fully *COMMITTED*!

1. The **commitment**, love, and dedication of Rizpah who spent weeks (night and day) protecting the bodies of her dead family. (2 Samuel 21)
    Question: Is there someone in my family who needs to be honored?
    Question: Is there someone in my life who requires my full attention?

2. Noah was **all-in**. He built an ark for 100+ years, because God found him a righteous and blameless man. He walked in God's grace. (Genesis 6)
    Question: Lord, is there someone to whom I need to grant grace?
    Prayer: Lord, empower me to walk rightly that I, like Noah, may find favor in your eyes.

3. Be **committed** like Isaiah, who said, "Here I am, send me." (Isaiah 6:8)
    Question: Lord, what commitments do you desire from me?
    Prayer: Lord, empower me to respond according to Your will.

4. Be **sold out** like Nehemiah, who wept, mourned, fasted, and prayed when he learned that the walls and gates of Jerusalem were broken down and burned. (Nehamiah 1:3-4)
    Question: Lord, does it break my heart to see broken places in Your church?
    Prayer: Lord, give me the empathy and will to repair broken places!

5. Desire the **_loyalty and commitment_** to the tenets of our faith like the other Mary and fellow-workers who refused to work on the Sabbath. (Matthew 28:1)
   Question: Lord, am I doing anything during worship or on Sunday that dishonors You?
   Prayer: Lord, help me to be totally dedicated to You.

6. Be able to **submit** like Mary (Virgin Mary) who said, "I am the Lord's servant; may it be to me as you have said." (Luke 1:38)
   Question: Lord, what area in my life have I not surrendered to You?
   Question: Lord, is there something I need to turn over to You?
   Prayer: Lord, give me the courage to obey Your instructions.

7. Paul lived in humble **submission** to Christ. He considered himself a slave of Jesus. (Philippians 1:1)
   Question: Lord, am I living in true submission?
   Question: In what ways can I trust and depend on You more?
   Question: How does my life show that I am a true disciple? Where do I have to improve?

QUESTION: What characteristics do you find common in most of these examples?

Lesson 6
Be a Living Sacrifice

"Present your bodies as a <u>living sacrifice</u>, holy and acceptable to God."
(from Romans 12:1)

A LIVING SACRIFICE

Romans 12:1-2 *I appeal to you therefore, brothers, by the mercies of God, to present your bodies as a **living sacrifice**, holy and acceptable to God, which is your spiritual worship. 2 Do not be conformed to this world, but be transformed by the renewal of your mind, that by testing you may discern what is the will of God, what is good and acceptable and perfect.* ESV

The message in this passage is that we are to offer spiritual sacrifices that honor and glorify God. Being a living sacrifice is a spiritual act of worship and we are to be transformed by renewing our minds (see also Psalm 119). Paul wants us to know God's will for our life and not be conformed to the world (1 John 2:15-17; James 4:4).

Jesus followers are to offer every part of their lives as an act of spiritual worship to God. Thus, worship is more than just music and singing – it's the lifestyle of a surrendered life. Every aspect of our lives should reflect the glory of God to the watching world. It means that we dedicate daily routines, work, and relationships to God. We fight the temptations of self-interest by submitting to His power and grace.

This passage serves as a call to total dedication in response to His mercy, emphasizing the transformative nature of true relationship with Him. The key points are:

- **Living Sacrifices**: Believers are urged to offer their lives as offerings that will be pleasing to God. This act of total surrender is seen as spiritual worship because our lives are dedicated to God.

    Our lives are to consist of prayer, worship, repentance, service to Christ, good deeds, taking up our cross, commitment to holiness, and loving one another deeply. This is further described by Peter:

    > **1 Peter 1:22-23** *Now that you have purified yourselves by obeying the truth so that you have sincere love for your brothers, love one another deeply, from the heart. For you have been born again, not of perishable seed, but of imperishable, through the living and enduring word of God.* NIV

- **Renewal of the Mind**: Disciples are called to reject worldly values and undergo a transformation through the renewal of their minds. Disciples are changed when they live a life committed to Christ.

- **Discern God's Will**: It's important to discern God's will. We should understand God's call on our life and be excited to live out His plan for our lives.

- **Being Good, Acceptable and Perfect:** Living this kind of life means a life of love according to the Great Commandment. Living a life of love is trying to imitate Jesus. We are to love God and one another with all our heart, mind, body, and soul. Imitating Christ results in loving others as yourself.

The appropriate response to God's grace is a life dedicated to Him; marked by worship, transformation, and discernment of His will. Unlike Old Testament sacrifices, this refers to an ongoing daily offering of living for God. The term spiritual worship likely means "reasonable service," implying that surrendering to God is the logical response to His mercy and grace.

Paul's audience in Rome would have been familiar with the sacrificial practices in both Jewish and pagan traditions. The concept of a "living sacrifice" would be understood as a call to continuous and complete dedication rather than a one-time religious act. True commitment to God means believers align their lives with His purposes.

OLD TESTAMENT SACRIFICES

Atonement is the act by which God restores a relationship to harmony and unity between Himself and human beings. This word can be broken into three parts which expresses a great truth in simple but profound terms: "at-one-ment."

In the Old Testament every sacrifice was assumed to be connected with the worshipper. Unless the heart accompanied the sacrifice, God rejected the gift (Isaiah 1:11, 13). The sin offering was first introduced by the law, the purpose of which was to make man conscious of sin. Every sacrifice was based on the concept of atonement, including the idea of the burnt offering. (Leviticus 1:4).[3]

In Israel, the sacrificial system operated for both the nation and the individual relative to the covenants between God and the Jewish nation. God provided the law and the covenants, which required sacrifices, but He also demanded that the people come before Him with clean hands and a pure heart.[4]

NEW TESTAMENT SACRIFICES

In the New Testament Jesus was the atoning sacrifice for our sins He became our sin offering paying our sin debt. Through God's atoning grace and forgiveness, we are reinstated to a relationship of at-one-ment with God. This is all in spite of our sin.[5]

In order to understand the concept of being a living sacrifice in the New Testament we will examine eight additional concepts that describe sacrifices for new covenant Jesus followers. We have already touched on Romans 12:1-2 above which clearly suggests giving our lives to God. This is confirmed in 2 Corinthians 8:5 where Paul says, "*And they did not do as we expected, but they gave themselves first to the Lord and then to us in keeping with God's will.*" (NIV) Let's look at the relative passages:

1. MY GIFTS (material alms)

Philippians 4:18 *I have received full payment and even more; I am amply supplied, now that I have received from Epaphroditus the gifts you sent. They are a fragrant offering, an acceptable sacrifice, pleasing to God.* NIV
Hebrews 13:16 *And do not forget to do good and to share with others, for with such sacrifices God is pleased.* NIV
Acts 10:4 *Cornelius stared at him in fear. "What is it, Lord?" he asked. The angel answered, "Your prayers and gifts to the poor have come up as a memorial offering before God."* NIV

In Philippians our gifts and offerings are described as fragrant and acceptable offerings that please God. These acts can be described as tangible expressions of love, generosity, and obedience to God's commands. Thus, a living sacrifice involves giving sacrificially, not out of obligation, but as an act of worship and gratitude. We are to cultivate a heart of generosity and cheerfully give to support the needs of others. The authentic Jesus follower recognizes giving as a spiritual act of worship.

Discussion Question:
1. How does giving deepen your faith and spiritual growth?

2. MY PRAISE

Hebrews 13:15 *Through Jesus, therefore, let us continually offer to God a <u>sacrifice of praise</u> – the fruit of lips that confess his name.* NIV

Here praise is described as a continual sacrifice of the "fruit of lips" that confess God's name. A living sacrifice involves worshiping God wholeheartedly and consistently, regardless of circumstances. The expected response of a Jesus follower is to offer consistent praise and gratitude to God, acknowledging His goodness and sovereignty.

Praise should flow naturally from a transformed heart and renewed mind. Peter does not use the description of a sacrifice but confirms the act of declaring praises to God in 1 Peter 2:9, *But you are . . . a people belonging to God, that you may declare the praises of him who called you out of darkness into his wonderful light.* NIV

Discussion Question:
2. Why do you think praise is described as a sacrifice?

3. MY SPIRITUAL SACRIFICES

1 Peter 2:5 *you also, like living stones, are being built into a spiritual house to be a holy priesthood, offering <u>spiritual sacrifices</u> acceptable to God through Jesus Christ.* NIV

Spiritual sacrifices can include prayer, worship, repentance, self-denying service to Christ, etc. Hebrews 10:14 tells us that through His sacrifice we are being made perfect and holy. Jesus followers are called to offer spiritual sacrifices that are acceptable to God, becoming part of His spiritual house and holy priesthood. Holy living is essential to being a living sacrifice because it reflects God's holiness. Thus, spiritual sacrifices are acts of obedience, service, and worship that honor Him.

Discussion Question:
3. How would you explain that your life can be a spiritual offering acceptable to God?

4. MY FAITH

Philippians 2:17 *But even if I am being poured out like a drink <u>offering</u> on the <u>sacrifice</u> and service coming from your faith, I am glad and rejoice with all of you.* NIV [see also Hebrews 11:4]
Hebrews 11:4 *<u>By faith</u> Abel offered God a <u>better sacrifice</u> than Cain did. By faith he was commended as a righteous man, when God spoke well of his <u>offerings</u>. And by faith he still speaks, even though he is dead.* NIV

Here faith means believing and accepting the truth of the Gospel. Faith is a vital component of sacrifice, illustrated by Abel's acceptable offering and Paul's description of himself as a drink offering. A living sacrifice is marked by unwavering faith and trust in God. A faithful Jesus follower trusts God's promises and aligns his actions with God's will. Thus, trials and sacrifices can become opportunities to glorify God.

Discussion Question:
4. How does your faith enable <u>you</u> to live sacrificially for God?

5. MY LOVE

Ephesians 5:2 *Walk in the way of love, just as Christ loved us and gave himself up for us as a <u>fragrant offering and sacrifice</u> to God.* NIV

John 13:34-35 *Love one another . . . By this everyone will know that you are my disciples, if you love one another.* NIV

Paul describes the nature of love as a sacrifice and John confirms the importance of love, although he does not describe it as a sacrifice or offering. Christ-like love demonstrates true discipleship. Jesus said, *"If you love me, keep my commands."* (John 14:15 NIV) Obedience is a non-negotiable aspect of discipleship. Love is described in Ephesians 5:2 as a fragrant offering, which is modeled after Christ's sacrificial love. Putting other's needs above self requires being a living sacrifice. We are to follow Christ's example by loving sacrificially and selflessly. Thus, we demonstrate love in tangible ways, even when it costs something.

Discussion Question:
5. What does sacrificial love look like to <u>you</u> in everyday life?

6. MY MERCY

Matthew 12:7 *If you had known what these words mean, 'I desire mercy, <u>not sacrifice</u>,' you would not have condemned the innocent.* NIV

Matthew 9:13 *But go and learn what this means: I desire mercy, <u>not sacrifice</u>." For I have not come to call the righteous, but sinners.* NIV

Mercy is prioritized over ritual animal sacrifices, emphasizing compassion over legalism. A living sacrifice practices mercy, which displays God's grace and kindness. Our response should be to show compassion and forgiveness. We should avoid judgmental attitudes and extend grace to others.

Discussion Question:
6. Why do <u>you</u> think God desires mercy over sacrifice?

7. MY PRAYER

Acts 10:4 *Your prayers and gifts to the poor have come up as a <u>memorial offering</u> before God.* NIV

Prayer is a spiritual offering that rises to God as a memorial. We, as living sacrifices should pray faithfully, aligning our will with God's desires. We should develop a consistent and heartfelt prayer life, praying with humility and thanksgiving.

Discussion Question:
7. How would <u>you</u> describe prayer as a form of sacrifice?

8. CONVERSION OF GENTILES / PROCLAIMING GOSPEL

Romans 15:16 *to be a minister of Christ Jesus to the Gentiles with the priestly duty of proclaiming the gospel of God, so that the Gentiles might become an <u>offering acceptable to God</u>.*

Proclaiming the gospel is likened to a priestly duty, with new converts being offerings to God. A living sacrifice actively participates in evangelism and discipleship. We are to share the gospel with others. It should be a joyful act of service to God.

Discussion Question:
8. How would you describe sharing the gospel as an act of sacrifice?

CONCLUSION

Being a living sacrifice as described in Romans 12:1-2 involves total devotion to Christ and is evidenced by material giving, praise, spiritual discipline, faith, love, mercy, prayer, and gospel proclamation. These faith acts demonstrate surrender and transformation, aligning every aspect of our lives with God's will. They move believers into a deeper relationship with God, allowing His glory to shine through our lives in powerful ways.

Our number one priority in life must be our relationship with Jesus. In order to be "right with God" we must be totally committed to our faith and living in accordance with His ways. We should fight to overcome any sin in our lives and follow the advice of Matthew 6:33 to seek first the kingdom of God.

God *does* want our continuing sacrifices in the form of what we do and how we live. The Old Testament clearly indicates that the animal sacrifices were not what God *really* wanted — He wanted changed lives:

> *You do not delight in sacrifice, or I would bring it; you do not take pleasure in burnt offerings. 17 The sacrifices of God are a broken spirit; a broken and contrite heart, O God, you will not despise.* (Psalm 51:16-17 NIV)

Therefore I cut you in pieces with my prophets, I killed you with the words of my mouth; my judgments flashed like lightning upon you. 6 For I desire mercy, not sacrifice, and acknowledgment of God rather than burnt offerings.
(Hosea 6:5-6 NIV)

Our reading in this lesson indicates God still wants sacrifices. Such sacrifices are clearly defined and very specific. They are also very encompassing as Romans 12:1 suggests we make our lives a living sacrifice.

DISCUSSION AND THOUGHT QUESTIONS

9. That does it mean to <u>you</u> to offer your body as a "living sacrifice" to God?

10. How do you think renewing of the mind leads to transformation? What practical steps can aid this process?

11. What are some patterns of this world that believers should avoid?

12. How do you think believers can discern God's "good, pleasing, and perfect will"?

13. Why do you think the New Testament writers refer to these acts as sacrifices or offerings? What are the writers trying to impress on us by using this language that obviously creates reference to Old Testament laws?

14. What must <u>you personally do</u> to conform to the following requirements of being a living sacrifice:

1. PRIORITY:

2. OBEDIENCE:

3. SIN:

4. SEEKING:

15. What is the result or benefit of a Jesus follower conforming to the following:

SPIRITUAL ACTS OF WORSHIP:

GIFTS:

PRAISE:

SPIRITUAL SACRIFICES:

FAITH:

LOVE:

MERCY:

16. What do <u>you</u> believe is the <u>most critical</u> challenge for being a living sacrifice? Explain.

GENERAL:

FOR ME:

17. What are <u>you</u> going to do about this subject in your life? What are your next steps?

Wisdom to Action
Challenge

In what specific way can you offer yourself as a "living sacrifice" to God this week? How might this act of worship transform your mindset or daily routine?

Lesson 7
Commit To Spiritual Growth

*If I get out of the boat, it had better be
anchored to Jesus, otherwise, when I
get back in, it may have drifted away.
I need to be anchored to a firm foundation
and know fully who is holding the anchor.*

WE MUST KNOW HIM

If our goal is to imitate Christ and walk in His ways, then we must know Him and understand His plan for our lives. We must acquaint ourselves with the sovereign majestic God who is the Creator of the heavens and earth. We should desire the peace that comes from knowing Him and seeking His ways.

How do we come to know God? The Bible says that we will begin to know Him if we are obedient to His commands, walk in His ways, and do what pleases Him. We are to love Him with all our heart, mind, and strength. We should make Him a priority in our lives. We should be seeking knowledge and understanding of His ways. We should be seeking Him on all occasions.

> The pure in heart are blessed and they will see God! Lord Jesus, give us the ability to be pure in heart so that we can see and know You. Help us understand that the values of this world are Satan's deceptions. Guide us in avoiding the cravings of this earthly life and the lusting after the things my eyes behold. Give me strength to seek after You and follow Your will. Amen!

SPIRITUAL GROWTH

Romans 8:29-30 *For those whom he foreknew he also predestined to be conformed to the image of his Son, in order that he might be the firstborn among many brothers.* ESV

Discipleship is a lifelong journey of spiritual growth in which we gradually become more like Jesus. We commit to learning His ways and obeying His commands. These commitments represent "guideposts" along our path of spiritual growth. Scripture has much to say about spiritual growth. For example:

> **Philippians 1:6** *And I am sure of this, that he who began a good work in you will bring it to completion at the day of Jesus Christ.* ESV

God is working in us providing ongoing growth and improvement rather than a quick achievement of perfection. We grow over time as the Holy Spirit guides our lives and development.

Jesus followers immerse themselves in Scripture in order to grow and shape their values, decisions, and behavior. The Word of God guards our way of living as confirmed in Psalm 119:9-11: *"How can a young man keep his way pure? By guarding it according to your word. 10 With my whole heart I seek you; let me not wander from your commandments! 11 I have stored up your word in my heart that I might not sin against you."* ESV

Paul tells us to let God's Word dwell richly in our hearts and guide our actions. In Colossians 3:16-17 he says, *"Let the word of Christ dwell in you richly, teaching and admonishing one another in all wisdom, singing psalms and hymns and spiritual songs, with thankfulness in your hearts to God. 17 And whatever you do, in word or deed, do everything in the name of the Lord Jesus, giving thanks to God the Father through him."* ESV

Scripture must be the foundation of our spiritual growth and daily lives. Knowledge of and understanding the instructions of God's Word must impact our lives such that we translate His Word into action and obedience. We do this by reading, studying, and memorizing Scripture, particularly those passages that address challenges in life.

A critical aspect of living by His Word is knowing it in order to develop understanding and wisdom. Peter confirms this in 2 Peter 1:5-8: *For this very reason, make every effort to supplement your faith with virtue, and virtue with knowledge, 6 and knowledge with self-control, and self-control with steadfastness, and steadfastness with godliness, 7 and godliness with brotherly affection, and brotherly affection with love. 8 For if these qualities are yours and are increasing, they keep you from being ineffective or unfruitful in the knowledge of our Lord Jesus Christ.* ESV

WARNINGS

Luke 13:24-25 *Strive to enter through the narrow door. For many, I tell you, will seek to enter and will not be able. 25 When once the master of the house has risen and shut the door, and you begin to stand outside and to knock at the door, saying, "Lord, open to us," then he will answer you, <u>"I do not know where you come from</u>."* ESV

Matt 25:10-12 *And while they were going to buy* [oil for the virgin's lamps], *the bridegroom came, and those who were ready went in with him to the marriage feast, and the door was shut. 11 Afterward the other virgins came also, saying, "Lord, lord, open to us." 12 But he answered, <u>"Truly, I say to you, I do not know you.</u>"* ESV

2 Thessalonians 1:7-8 *Grant relief to you who are afflicted as well as to us, when the Lord Jesus is revealed from heaven with his mighty angels 8 in flaming fire, <u>inflicting vengeance on those who do not know God</u> and on those who do not obey the gospel of our Lord Jesus.* ESV

Knowing is important.
It can be a matter of life and death!

KNOWLEDGE OF GOD

The best advice for anyone seeking the knowledge of God is to zealously meditate on and study His Word regularly. We must call on our inner nature to have continual engagement with His Word. Ideally it should be daily in a time and place where we are alone and have time to think and ponder over the words and meaning of Scripture.

Solomon's notable proverb tells us of the value of finding the knowledge of God:

> **Proverbs 2:1-6** *My son, if you accept my words and store up my commands within you, turning your ear to wisdom and applying your heart to understanding—indeed, if you call out for insight and cry aloud for understanding, and if you look for it as for silver and search for it as for hidden treasure, then you will understand the fear of the LORD and find the knowledge of God. For the LORD gives wisdom; from his mouth come knowledge and understanding.* NIV

This passage highlights that understanding and applying God's Word requires intentional effort—listening, seeking, and valuing it as one would treasure gold. It emphasizes diligence in studying Scripture. True wisdom originates from God, reinforcing the truth that believers must rely on Him for understanding, not just human effort or intellect.

Reverence for God ("fear of the Lord") is foundational for gaining spiritual insight and understanding His Word. Studying Scripture is not passive but rather a disciplined pursuit that leads to a deeper relationship with God.

Paul tells us further that Scripture equips us for every good work: "*All Scripture is breathed out by God and profitable for teaching, for reproof, for correction, and for training in righteousness, 17 that the man of God may be competent, equipped for every good work.*" (2 Timothy 3:16-17 ESV) This is consistent with the well-known Psalm from the Old Testament:

"Your word is a lamp to my feet and a light to my path." (Psalm 119:105 ESV)

The Key to Understanding and Wisdom

The nature of what we want to accomplish can be illustrated by the reference to the Bereans in Acts 17. Paul was in Thessalonica and had spent three Sabbath days teaching in the synagogue. The text says that he "reasoned with them from the Scriptures," explaining how Jesus (the Messiah) had to suffer and rise from the dead. Paul wanted the people to recognize that Jesus was their long awaited Messiah. Some of the listeners were persuaded, including some influential people. That upset some other Jews, so they stirred up the people and threatened Paul and his friends, particularly Jason with whom Paul was staying.

Paul and Silas were sent off to Berea where they immediately went to the local synagogue. The text does not indicate whether the Bereans knew about the events in Thessalonica, but it would be likely they were aware of the controversy that Paul had created with his teaching. However, the Bereans' response to Paul was much more reasoned. The text says they were open-minded and eager to hear what Paul had to say, and rather than reacting without reason they "examined the Scriptures daily to see if these things were correct."

There is a great lesson herein. Don't trust the words of man until you have verified them with the words of God. Recently someone in my small group said, "God helps those who help themselves." They thought they were quoting Scripture in response to a discussion concerning man's responsibility to his faith. The problem is that this quote is not in the Bible. It may be good advice at times, but it is not Scripture. We must know the Word well enough to know when someone is misleading us, even when it is not intentional.

We must be prepared in season and out of season to respond to questions and inquiries about what we believe and what the

Bible says on certain subjects. We included Matthew 25:10-12 above about the virgins who needed more oil for their lamps because they came unprepared! We cannot afford to come to our faith unprepared.

In Matthew 25 Jesus describes what the kingdom of heaven will be like. He told a story or parable about ten virgins who came out to wait on the coming groom so they could announce his arrival to the bride. There were five foolish virgins who did not bring any extra oil for their lamps. When they ran low they asked the five who were prepared to borrow some oil. The answer was no! The unprepared were told to go buy more oil but when they returned the groom had already come and all had entered the wedding banquet. The door was closed and there was no place for the five who had been unprepared!

Focus here on what is being taught! Jesus began the story by describing the kingdom of heaven. The virgins who returned from buying oil knocked and asked to be let into the banquet, but the Master said, "I assure you, I do not know you." The passage ends with the warning, "Therefore be alert, because you don't know either the time or the day or the hour."

That is a pretty sobering thought! It should cause us to ask ourselves, "Do I know the important facts about my faith? Am I prepared for the Master to return?" What if the Master would ask you, "Why should I let you in?" Would you have an answer? You will know the answers to these types of questions if you are reading and studying the Word of God on a regular basis.

COMMIT TO KNOWING GOD's WORD

Psalm 107:20 *He sent out his word and healed them, and delivered them from their destruction.* ESV

> God's Word is a source of healing and deliverance. It carries life-saving power, both physically and spiritually. Committing to God's Word allows us to experience restoration and rescue from spiritual danger.

Psalm 147:18 *He sends out his word, and melts them; he makes his wind blow and the waters flow.* ESV

> God's Word has transformative power, illustrated by its ability to control creation (melting ice or stirring waters). Knowing God's Word enables us to witness and trust in His power to change both the natural and spiritual realms.

Isaiah 40:8 *The grass withers, the flower fades, but the word of our God will stand forever.* ESV

> God's Word is eternal and unchanging, unlike the fleeting nature of human life and earthly matters. Committing to Scripture gives us a firm foundation and an eternal perspective in a transient world.

Isaiah 55:11 *My word that goes out from my mouth; it shall not return to me empty, but it shall accomplish that which I purpose, and shall succeed in the thing for which I sent it.* ESV

> God's Word is purposeful; it never fails to achieve the goal for which it was sent. Knowing Scripture ensures alignment with God's plans, which will always come to fruition.

Galatians 3:8 *And the Scripture, foreseeing that God would justify the Gentiles by faith, preached the gospel beforehand to Abraham, saying, "In you shall all the nations be blessed."* ESV

> God's Word contains His redemptive plan which will culminate in the blessing of all nations through faith in Christ. Committing to Scripture allows us to understand and share the grand narrative of God's salvation for humanity.

Ephesians 5:26 *that he might sanctify her, having cleansed her by the washing of water with the word.* ESV

> God's Word has a sanctifying and cleansing effect, purifying believers and preparing them for holiness. Regular immersion in God's Word transforms our hearts and lives, enabling us to grow in holiness.

Hebrews 4:12-13 *For the word of God is living and active, sharper than any two-edged sword, piercing to the division of soul and of spirit, of joints and of marrow, and discerning the thoughts and intentions of the heart. 13 And no creature is hidden from his sight, but all are naked and exposed to the eyes of him to whom we must give account.* ESV

God's Word is alive, dynamic, and penetrating. It has the power to expose the deepest thoughts and motives of the heart. This makes a commitment to Scripture essential for self-examination and spiritual growth. Knowing God's Word helps us discern right from wrong and prepares us for accountability before God.

1 John 2:14 *I write to you, fathers, because you know him who is from the beginning. I write to you, young men, because you are strong, and the word of God abides in you, and you have overcome the evil one.* ESV

God's Word strengthens believers, enabling them to overcome sin and the schemes of the enemy. Commitment to Scripture equips us with the strength and wisdom to resist temptation and walk in victory.

Psalm 19:7-9 *The law of the Lord is perfect, reviving the soul; the testimony of the Lord is sure, making wise the simple; 8 the precepts of the Lord are right, rejoicing the heart; the commandment of the Lord is pure, enlightening the eyes; 9 the fear of the Lord is clean, enduring forever; the rules of the Lord are true, and righteous altogether.* ESV

God's Word is perfect, trustworthy, righteous, and life-giving. It revives the soul, grants wisdom, brings joy, and provides enlightenment. By committing to God's Word, we access its transformative power for spiritual renewal.

SUMMARY: Committing to God's Word

- **God's Word is alive and eternal:** It penetrates the heart (Hebrews 4:12), is unchanging (Isaiah 40:8), and endures forever (Psalm 19).

- **God's Word is powerful and purposeful:** It brings healing (Psalm 107:20), achieves God's plans (Isaiah 55:11), and sanctifies believers (Ephesians 5:26).

- **God's Word equips believers:** It provides wisdom (Psalm 19:7-9), strengthens for spiritual victory (1 John 2:14), and reveals God's salvation plan (Galatians 3:8).

A commitment to knowing God's Word is essential for experiencing spiritual transformation, living victoriously, and participating in God's redemptive work in the world. God's Word is not only instructive – it will heal and save. It can also protect us from foolishness and the Evil One who would misuse His Word to trick and trap us. These characteristics of God's Word should encourage us to saturate our hearts and minds with His words and instructions.

BENEFITS OF GOD's WORD

It's divinely inspired:
2 Peter 1:20-21 *Above all, you must understand that no prophecy of Scripture came about by the prophet's own interpretation of things. For prophecy never had its origin in the human will, but prophets, though human, spoke from God as they were carried along by the Holy Spirit.*

This passage affirms that Scripture is not a product of human creativity or interpretation but is divinely inspired by the Holy Spirit. It underscores the active role of the Holy Spirit in guiding human authors, ensuring that Scripture is authoritative and trustworthy.

Readers are reminded to approach Scripture with humility, recognizing that it requires discernment and guidance, as its meaning originates with God, not man. This passage reinforces the authority, reliability, and divine inspiration of Scripture, encouraging believers to approach it with reverence and trust in its truth.

Jesus fulfills Scripture:
Matthew 5:17-18 *Do not think that I have come to abolish the Law or the Prophets; I have not come to abolish them but to fulfill them. For truly I tell you, until heaven and earth disappear, not the smallest letter, not the least stroke of a pen, will by any means disappear from the Law until everything is accomplished.* (NIV)

Jesus affirms the enduring relevance and authority of the Old Testament Scriptures, showing that they remain foundational even under the New Testament. Jesus fulfills the Law and the Prophets through His life, death, and resurrection, completing their purpose and revealing their ultimate meaning. The permanence of God's Word is emphasized—it remains until all is fulfilled, indicating its ongoing applicability and reliability. Believers are called to honor the entirety of God's Word, understanding that Jesus fulfills its promises and commands, making Scripture a unified and eternal revelation.

Together, these two passages deepen our appreciation for the reliability and eternal nature of God's Word. Thus we can be comfortable in applying it in our lives.

VALUE OF GOD's WORD: Psalm 119

The author of Psalm 119 reveals profound truths about the value of God's Word, emphasizing its indispensable role in the believer's life. There are a number of important truths in Psalm 119. These ten key teachings about the value of God's Word are worth remembering:

1. God's Word is a Source of Life and Revival

In Psalm 119:25, 50, 93 the psalmist repeatedly acknowledges that God's Word revives the soul and gives life in times of distress or spiritual dryness. God's Word is not static but dynamic, offering encouragement and restoration to those who seek it.

2. God's Word is a Guide for Righteous Living

Psalm 119:9, 105, and 130 tell us that the Word serves as a lamp to our feet and a light to our path, providing direction for living a life of holiness and wisdom. Scripture allows believers to discern the right way to live and avoid the pitfalls of sin and confusion.

3. God's Word is a Source of Joy and Delight

Psalm 119:14, 16, 111 indicate that there is more joy and satisfaction in God's Word than in worldly wealth and pleasures. Immersing oneself in Scripture brings lasting delight and fulfillment that material possessions cannot provide.

4. God's Word is Trustworthy and Eternal

In Psalm 119:42, 89 and 160 God's Word is firmly fixed in heaven, enduring for all generations. It is trustworthy and true, offering a solid foundation for our faith. Believers can confidently rely on God's Word, knowing it will never fail or become obsolete. Trusting His Word involves confidence in its truth and reliability, even in the face of doubt or opposition. It is the ultimate source of guidance and hope.

5. God's Word Provides Strength and Comfort in Trials

In Psalm 119:28, 50, and 92 the psalmist finds strength in God's promises during suffering and acknowledges that Scripture sustains him when life becomes overwhelming. In times of hardship, God's Word is a source of hope and strength.

6. God's Word is a Tool for Moral and Spiritual Purity

In Psalm 119:9 and 11 we learn that by treasuring God's Word we can remain pure and avoid sin. Scripture equips believers to resist temptation and live in alignment with God's standards.

7. God's Word is to Be Treasured

Psalm 119:15, 72, 97, and 127 tell us that we should treasure God's Word more than gold and continually meditate on its truths, because in it we find wisdom and guidance. Valuing Scripture and reflecting on it regularly leads to spiritual growth and intimacy with God. Treasuring His Word means we recognize its value compared to worldly possessions.

8. God's Word Leads to Wisdom and Understanding

In verses 98 to 100 and 130 the psalmist declares that God's Word makes him wiser than his enemies, teachers, and elders. It brings understanding to the simple. Knowledge and understanding of Scripture can develop spiritual insight that surpasses worldly knowledge.

9. God's Word Invites Love and Obedience

Psalm 119:47, 48, and 97 express deep love for God's commandments and a desire for obedience. Our love for God naturally leads to a desire to live out His Word in daily life.

10. God's Word Requires Active Engagement

Finally Psalm 119:15, 18, and 33 to 34 tell us to commit to meditating on, learning, and seeking deeper understanding of His Word. A serious commitment to study and apply God's Word is essential for spiritual maturity. Seeking knowledge should be a lifelong pursuit for understanding and wisdom. It requires humility to recognize there is always more to learn. Disciples engage in consistent Bible study seeking insight from teachers, commentaries, and mentors to deepen their understanding.

Conclusion: Value of God's Word (Psalm 119)

Psalm 119 is a profound meditation on the importance of God's Word, emphasizing its role in guiding, sustaining, and transforming the lives of those who follow Him. The psalm uses nearly every verse to express devotion to God's statutes, laws, decrees, precepts, commands, and promises, painting a comprehensive picture of how essential God's Word is to a believer's life.

It teaches us that His Word is a treasure of unmatched worth, a guide for righteous living, and a source of strength, wisdom, and joy. The result of such devotion is a life marked by peace and intimacy with God. God's Word not only shapes our present journey but anchors us in eternal truth. The result of following God's Word is described as:

- **Purity:** Living by God's Word helps believers maintain a pure heart (v. 9).
- **Peace:** Great peace is granted to those who love His law (v. 165).
- **Strength and Endurance:** The Word sustains believers through trials and afflictions (vv. 25, 92).
- **Guidance:** It serves as a lamp to our feet and a light to our path (v. 105).
- **Joy:** Obedience brings delight and satisfaction (vv. 16, 111).
- **Hope and Salvation:** His promises give assurance of both hope and salvation for the future (vv. 41, 81).

Psalm 119 encourages believers to approach God's Word with reverence and commitment. By meditating on and obeying God's Word, we grow in intimacy with God and demonstrate our genuine faith.

__God's Word can transform Your life.__

HOW TO USE GOD's WORD

The following verses emphasize the transformative power of engaging with God's Word. They encourage a wholehearted approach to Scripture: internalizing and living by its precepts.

Meditate On It:
Joshua 1:8 *Keep this Book of the Law always on your lips; meditate on it day and night, so that you may be careful to do everything written in it. Then you will be prosperous and successful.* NIV

> Meditation on God's Word ensures that His truth saturates our hearts and minds, leading to spiritual alignment with His will. It emphasizes continuous engagement with Scripture, suggesting that success and prosperity in life, especially spiritual success, is tied to obedience.

Believe It:
Luke 24:25 *He said to them, "How foolish you are, and how slow to believe all that the prophets have spoken!"* NIV

> Jesus rebukes His followers for their slowness to believe Scripture. It underscores the importance of trusting the promises and warnings of Scripture. Doubt or rebellion can hinder our spiritual understanding.

Obey It:
John 14:21 *Whoever has my commands and keeps them is the one who loves me. The one who loves me will be loved by my Father, and I too will love them and show myself to them.* NIV

> This verse ties obedience to a love relationship with Jesus. True love for God is expressed through obedience to His commands. It highlights a reciprocal relationship: when believers obey God's Word, they experience deeper intimacy with Him. Obedience is not merely a duty but a demonstration of a personal connection with Christ.

Psalm 119:1 instructs us to live according to the law of the Lord and Psalm 119:4 confirms that God's precepts are to be fully obeyed. God's Word is not just for understanding but guidance for obedient action (intentional adherence). We are to make practical commitments to align our actions with biblical principles in all aspects of our lives.

Study it Regularly:
Acts 17:11 *Now the Berean Jews were of more noble character than those in Thessalonica, for they received the message with great eagerness and examined the Scriptures every day to see if what Paul said was true.* NIV

The writer of Acts, Luke, commended the Bereans for their diligence in studying Scripture daily. Their eagerness and commitment serve as a model for believers. This verse emphasizes the importance of grounding faith and action in Scripture, ensuring that teachings and doctrines align with God's truth.

Teach It To Others:
Colossians 3:16 *Let the message of Christ dwell among you richly as you teach and admonish one another with all wisdom through psalms, hymns, and songs from the Spirit, singing to God with gratitude in your hearts.* NIV

This verse calls believers to not only internalize God's Word but also share it with others. Teaching and admonishing in wisdom help the body of Christ grow together in maturity and understanding. It reminds believers that Scripture is meant to be lived out and shared in both formal teaching and everyday conversations.

Psalm 119:13 and 46 tell us to share God's Word with others in order to demonstrate its power in our life and to encourage others in their faith journey.

Delight in It:
Psalm 1:2 *But his delight is in the law of the LORD, and on his law he meditates day and night.* NIV

We are called to find joy and satisfaction in God's Word. Delight develops a heart of worship and gratitude.

Memorize It:
Psalm 119:11 *I have hidden your word in my heart that I might not sin against you.* NIV

Memorizing Scripture equips believers to recall God's truths in difficult times, to resist temptation, and to encourage others when appropriate.

Speak It:
Deuteronomy 6:6-7 *These commandments that I give you today are to be on your hearts. Impress them on your children. Talk about them when you sit at home and when you walk along the road, when you lie down and when you get up.* NIV

Speaking God's Word reinforces it in our own hearts and passes it on to the next generation.

Live It (Apply It):
James 1:22 *Do not merely listen to the word, and so deceive yourselves. Do what it says.* NIV

True engagement with God's Word requires action. Applying Scripture to our lives transforms followers and reflects genuine discipleship to others.

Defend It:
2 Peter 3:15 *Always be prepared to give an answer to everyone who asks you to give the reason for the hope that you have. But do this with gentleness and respect.* NIV

Believers must uphold and defend the truth of God's Word, sharing it with confidence when questioned.

DISCUSSION QUESTIONS

Spiritual Growth

1. What does spiritual growth mean to you personally and how do you know when you're growing spiritually?

2. What are some barriers that can hinder spiritual growth and how can we overcome them?

3. How does consistent engagement with God's Word contribute to spiritual growth?

4. How does being part of a Christian community or small group contribute to spiritual growth?

Knowing God's Word

5. Why is God's Word described as "living and active" in Hebrews 4:12? How does this description influence your view of studying the Bible?

6. In Joshua 1:8, God instructs Joshua to meditate on the Word day and night. How does meditating on Scripture differ from just reading it? What benefits does it bring?

7. Why does the psalmist in Psalm 119:11 say he hides God's Word in his heart? How can memorizing Scripture be helpful?

8. In Acts 17:11, the Bereans are commended for eagerly examining the Scriptures daily. What can we learn from their example about the importance of studying the Bible?

9. How does knowing and studying God's Word strengthen our faith and help us face doubts or challenges (Romans 10:17)?

10. What are some common distractions or obstacles that prevent us from studying and learning God's Word? How can we overcome these challenges?

Psalm 119

11. The psalmist repeatedly expresses love for God's Word (e.g., Psalm 119:97, 127). What does it mean to "love" God's Word? How can we cultivate that emotion or core value in our daily lives?

12. In Psalm 119:165, the psalmist says, "Great peace have those who love your law, and nothing can make them stumble." How does knowing and following God's Word bring peace and stability to life?

13. In what ways does Psalm 119 portray God's Word as vital for every aspect of life—spiritual, emotional, and practical? How have you experienced this in your own life?

Wisdom to Action
Challenge

Identify an area of spiritual stagnation in your life. What concrete step can you take to actively pursue growth in this area and bear fruit for God's kingdom?

Lesson 8
Serve Others and Produce Fruit

"By their fruit you will recognize them. Do people pick grapes from thorn bushes, or figs from thistles? Likewise, every good tree bears good fruit, but a bad tree bears bad fruit. A good tree cannot bear bad fruit, and a bad tree cannot bear good fruit."
Matthew 7:16-18 (NIV)

BEARING FRUIT

The concept of "bearing fruit" in a biblical context is a metaphor that describes how a person's life can show evidence of their faith and relationship with God. Let's break down what this term means:

What is "Fruit"?

In the Bible "fruit" refers to the good things that come from or result from a person's connection to God. This can include good deeds (helping others, being kind, and serving those in need). It can also refer to character traits like love, joy, peace, patience, kindness, and self-control, which are often referred to as the "fruit of the Spirit" (Galatians 5:22-23).

Source of Fruitfulness

Just like a tree needs healthy roots and good soil to produce fruit, a person needs to be connected to God in order to bear spiritual fruit. Jesus describes Himself as the "vine" and His followers as the "branches" (John 15:5). This means we are to:

- **Stay connected to Jesus:** To bear fruit, one must maintain a close relationship with Jesus, much like branches rely on the vine for nourishment.

- **Depend on God:** It's not about trying hard on our own but about allowing God to work in us and through us.

Importance

Bearing fruit is important because it demonstrates the impact of faith in a person's life. It shows that a person is living out his beliefs and making a positive difference in the world. Jesus said that good fruit is a sign of a healthy relationship with Him and that it brings glory to God (John 15:8).

How accomplished?

To bear fruit believers may engage various spiritual disciplines in order to deepen their understanding of God and His will for their lives. Followers can serve others by looking for opportunities to help and support those in need. These activities will require developing qualities like patience and kindness in everyday interactions and relationships.

Summary

"Bearing fruit" is thus about living a life that reflects one's faith through good actions and positive character traits, all made possible by a close relationship with God. It's a way to show the world the love and goodness that comes from following Jesus. A Jesus follower who bears fruit will have a life marked by abiding in Christ and serving others, all evidence of a spiritual relationship that impacts God's kingdom.

BEARING FRUIT vs. SERVING

Serving is the process or means by which we bear fruit. When we humbly serve we bear fruit that impacts the lives of others. Teaching a Bible study may result in people growing spiritually (bearing fruit). Sharing the gospel could lead to someone coming to faith in Christ (bearing fruit).

Bearing fruit is the result or evidence of faithful service. If our service is done in obedience to God and empowered by the Holy Spirit, it will produce spiritual fruit. For example, a church ministry that serves the needs of others will lead to deeper community relationships and ultimately more people accepting Jesus as Savior and Lord (fruit).

This process might be illustrated further by recognizing that the service is planting, watering, and nurturing the tree, while the fruit is the harvest or the result of that nurturing process. The concepts of "bearing fruit" and "serving" are closely related but distinct in emphasis and result. Both are essential aspects of a committed Jesus follower's life.

Key Verses

Bearing Fruit
John 15:4-8 *Remain in me, as I also remain in you . . . I am the vine; you are the branches. If you remain in me and I in you, you will bear much fruit; apart from me you can do nothing . . . This is to my Father's glory, that you bear much fruit, showing yourselves to be my disciples.* (NIV)

Abiding in Christ is essential for spiritual growth and effectiveness. A fruitful life reflects dependence on Christ and commitment to His purposes.

Serving
Matthew 20:26 *Whoever wants to become great among you must be your servant.* NIV
1 Peter 4:10 *As each has received a gift, use it to serve one another, as good stewards of God's varied grace.* ESV

Serving refers to actively employing one's God-given time, talents, and resources to meet the needs of others. It reflects Christ's humility and love. Serving focuses on action and obedience in order to meet practical needs (feeding the hungry, helping the poor). It also includes ministering to others (teaching, encouraging, counseling, helping).

Focus
Galatians 5:22-23 *The fruit of the Spirit is love, joy, peace, forbearance, kindness, goodness, faithfulness, gentleness and self-control.* NIV

The key point here is that a fully committed disciple reflects the character of Christ.

Motivation

Both serving and bearing Fruit are motivated by the desire to bring glory to God and demonstrate a life transformed by Him. John 15:8 says, *"This is to my Father's glory, that you bear much fruit, showing yourselves to be my disciples."* (NIV). Thus, it's about being connected to Christ. John 15:5 says, *"If you remain in me and I in you, you will bear much fruit"* NIV.

Comparison

Aspect	Bearing Fruit	Serving
Focus	Outcome, evidence, results	Action, effort, and obedience
Measurement	Spiritual growth, impact on others	Faithful use of gifts and opportunities
Primary Purpose	Glorify God and reflect Christ	Meet needs, glorify God through service
Dependency	Requires abiding in Christ (John 15:5)	Requires humility and obedience
Duration	Long-term evidence, eternal impact	Immediate, practical expression of love

Summary

We have spent time talking about the difference between serving and bearing fruit because we can serve without bearing fruit. Service done with selfish motives, in one's own strength, or disconnected from Christ may not result in spiritual fruit. For example if we are serving to be seen by others there may be no fruit. (Matthew 6:1) A Christ-transformed life will normally overflow in loving others. A Jesus follower bears fruit as a result of serving *faithfully and abiding* in Christ.

Serving is <u>what we do</u>. It is the practical result of love and humility. Bearing fruit is <u>what God produces</u> through us because of our connection to Him. Serving is an active expression of our faith, while bearing fruit is the outcome God generates to bring glory to Himself. As we serve faithfully God produces fruit. To be both a servant and a fruitful follower of Jesus, we must abide in Christ (John 15:5) and faithfully steward what God has entrusted to us (Matthew 25:14-30).

Fruitfulness is sometimes misunderstood as mere success or participation in ministry. Biblically, being fruitful encompasses three concepts:

- **Transformation** (Fruit of the Spirit – Galatians. 5:22).
- **Good works** (Ephesians 2:10).
- **Impact on others** through love and service (John 13:34-35).

Jesus' teaching clarifies that obedience flows from a heart transformed by grace, not from earning salvation. It involves submission to God's commands, alignment with His purposes, and dependence on His Spirit for guidance.

True followers of Jesus are recognized not by their words but by their transformed lives which is indicated by their obedience, service, and love. The ultimate purpose of discipleship is to bring glory to the Father, demonstrated through a life that reflects His character and fulfills His mission. Obedience is not about legalistic serving but about living out a relationship with Christ that produces fruit empowered by the Holy Spirit

DISCUSSION QUESTIONS

1. What does "bearing much fruit" mean in John 15:8? How can we identify spiritual fruit in our lives?

2. How do we reconcile the idea of salvation by grace with the need to bear fruit as evidence of faith?

3. Why do you think Jesus warns against calling Him "Lord" without obedience? How can we avoid this pitfall?

4. What modern cultural attitudes make it difficult to bear fruit? How can believers overcome them?

5. How can we help fellow believers bear fruit?

MATTHEW 25:14-30 – The Parable of the Talents

For it will be like a man going on a journey, who called his servants and entrusted to them his property. 15 To one he gave five talents, to another two, to another one, to each according to his ability. Then he went away. 16 He who had received the five talents went at once and traded with them, and he made five talents more. 17 So also he who had the two talents made two talents more. 18 But he who had received the one talent went and dug in the ground and hid his master's money. 19 Now after a long time the master of those servants came and settled accounts with them. 20 And he who had received the five talents came forward, bringing five talents more, saying, 'Master, you delivered to me five talents; here I have made five talents more.' 21 His master said to him, 'Well done, good and faithful servant. You have been faithful over a little; I will set you over much. Enter into the joy of your master.' 22 And he also who had the two talents came forward, saying, 'Master, you delivered to me two talents; here I have made two talents more.' 23 His master said to him, 'Well done, good and faithful servant. You have been faithful over a little; I will set you over much. Enter into the joy of your master.' 24 He also who had received the one talent came forward, saying, 'Master, I knew you to be a hard man, reaping where you did not sow, and gathering where you scattered no seed, 25 so I was afraid, and I went and hid your talent in the ground. Here you have what is yours.' 26 But his master answered him, 'You wicked and slothful servant! You knew that I reap where I have not sowed and gather where I scattered no seed? 27 Then you ought to have invested my money with the bankers, and at my coming I should have received what was my own with interest. 28 So take the talent from him and give it to him who has the ten talents. 29 For to everyone who has will more be given, and he will have an abundance. But from the one who has not, even what he has will be taken away. 30 And cast the worthless servant into the outer darkness. In that place there will be weeping and gnashing of teeth. ESV

NOTE: The word "talent" (v. 15) originally referred to a large sum of money (equivalent to about 20 years of wages). However, in application, it symbolizes any resource God entrusts to us—skills, time, opportunities, or spiritual gifts. Other challenging phrases in the text include "outer darkness" and "weeping and gnashing of teeth" (v. 30). These terms symbolize separation from God and eternal loss, highlighting the severe consequences of unfaithfulness.

The Parable of the Talents teaches that Jesus' followers are entrusted with gifts, abilities, and opportunities to serve God. The "talents" represent resources, time, and spiritual or practical abilities. The master entrusts his servants with varying amounts, demonstrating his understanding of their abilities. The two faithful servants multiply what they've been given, while the third servant buries his talent out of fear or laziness.

The important messages of this passage are:

- God entrusts each person with gifts and opportunities (v. 14-15).
- Faithfulness in using what God has given brings reward and commendation (v. 21, 23). Rewards are based on effort and faithfulness, not result.
- Failure to use God-given abilities due to fear, laziness, or indifference leads to loss and judgment (v. 26-30).

The master-servant relationship dynamic was common in Jesus' day and illustrates God's authority and our accountability to Him. Servants often managed their master's wealth and were expected to increase it. Culturally, investing money involved risk, but avoiding risk (like burying the talent) was often seen as wasteful and unproductive. In a kingdom context, faithfulness to God involves actively using what He has given us. This should occur even when it requires stepping out in faith.

CORE MESSAGE – Parable of the Talents

The central message of this parable is that of *faithful stewardship.* God expects believers to actively use the gifts, talents, and opportunities He has given them for the benefit of His kingdom. These requirements align with other New Testament teachings to bear fruit (John 15:8), serve Christ (Ephesians 2:10, and prove yourself faithful (I Corinthians 4:2). The Parable of the Talents contrasts one being passive with those who are in active service. It emphasizes the eternal consequences of failing to act. Let me repeat, the problem which the third servant is that he failed or refused to serve.

Theological Themes

Stewardship is an important concept in the New Testament. Because everything we have belongs to God, we are accountable for how we use it. God desires and rewards faithful service, not outcomes. The first two servants receive the same commendation, despite different amounts of increase. The passage also reflects eternal consequences—faithful service leads to joy and reward, while passivity (refusal) leads to loss. These themes reinforce that serving and bearing fruit are essential components of a committed Jesus follower's life.

Practical Application

- **Know Your Gifts**: We should know and use the talents, skills, and opportunities God has entrusted to us.
- **Be Faithful with Small Things**: Start using your gifts, no matter how small. God honors faithfulness in little things (Luke 16:10).
- **Take Spiritual Risks**: Step out of your comfort zone to serve others if necessary.
- **Avoid Passivity**: Don't "bury" your talents out of fear, laziness, or false excuses.
- **Serve for God's Glory**: Use your talents to honor God, not for personal gain or recognition.

DISCUSSION QUESTIONS: Parable of the Talents

6. What do the talents in the parable represent, and what talents has God entrusted to you?

7. Why do you think the master praised the first two servants equally, even though they produced different results? What does this teach us about faithfulness?

8. What does this parable teach about the consequences of neglecting the gifts God has given us? How should this challenge us to take action?

9. How can we apply the concept of "faithful stewardship" in our daily lives? What are practical ways to use what God has given us? What does it mean for you personally?

10. The faithful servants took risks. What risks might God be asking you to take for His kingdom?

11. How can we encourage one another to develop and use our God-given talents effectively?

12. In what areas of your life do you sense God calling you to be more faithful or productive? What steps can you take this week to respond?

OTHER SIGNIFICANT TEACHINGS

There are other significant stories, parables, and teachings in the New Testament that emphasize serving others or producing fruit that are comparable to the Parable of the Talents:

1. The Parable of the Sheep and the Goats (Matthew 25:31-46)

> This parable directly follows the Parable of the Talents in Mathew. It emphasizes the importance of serving others as a reflection of serving Christ. Jesus separated people into two groups—sheep (righteous) and goats (unrighteous)—based on whether they provided acts of compassion like feeding the hungry, clothing the naked, visiting the sick, or caring for strangers. Serving others, especially the marginalized, is a sign of genuine faith and obedience to Christ. Neglecting to serve other's leads to judgment.

2. The Parable of the Good Samaritan (Luke 10:25-37)

> In response to a question about "Who is my neighbor?" Jesus told the story of a Samaritan who stopped to care for a wounded man when other religious people (a priest and a Levite) passed by. The Samaritan showed compassion, tended to the man's wounds, and ensured his continued care. True service may involve sacrificial love and crossing boundaries to help others in need, regardless of cultural differences. Serving others is not optional for a committed Jesus follower because service demonstrates God's love.

3. The Parable of the Workers in the Vineyard (Matthew 20:1-16)

> Jesus told the story of a landowner who hired workers at different times of the day but payed them all the same wage. Those who worked the longest grumbled, but the landowner reminded them of his generosity. God's grace and reward are not based on human ideas of fairness but on

His generosity. Serving in God's kingdom is a privilege, regardless of the timing or scale of one's work. All service in God's kingdom is valuable and we are called to serve faithfully without comparing ourselves to others.

4. Jesus Washed the Disciples' Feet (John 13:1-17)

At the Last Supper, Jesus performed the lowly task of washing His disciples' feet, teaching them that true leadership and greatness come through serving others. He instructed them to follow His example. Humble sacrificial service is the mark of a Jesus follower. Stop and consider what happened here! Jesus, our God, Lord, and Savior stooped to wash your feet!

5. The Parable of the Prodigal Son (Luke 15:11-32)

A son demanded his inheritance, squandered it, and later returned home in repentance. The father lovingly welcomed him back and celebrated his return. The older brother struggled with resentment over the father's grace and forgiveness. God's heart for restoration, grace, and forgiveness challenge us to serve others with a similar attitude. Serving others includes extending grace, forgiveness, and hospitality.

Summary

These parables share common themes with the Parable of the Talents:

- **Faithful Stewardship**: Using what God has given us (gifts, time, or resources) to serve Him and others.

- **Active Obedience**: Fruitfulness is the result of faithful obedience to Christ and living out His commands.

- **Compassion and Sacrifice**: Serving others may require humility, inconvenience, and a willingness to meet the needs of others as Christ did.

These examples challenge Jesus followers to take their commitment to serving and bearing fruit seriously, recognizing that our service reflects our love for God and fulfills His purposes.

DISCUSSION AND THOUGHT QUESTIONS

13. Why does Jesus emphasize serving others as a mark of discipleship? (John 13:14-17, Matthew 25:40)

14. How does serving others also serve God? (Matthew 25:40, Colossians 3:23-24)

15. What are some practical ways we can identify and use the talents, gifts, and resources God has given us? (Matthew 25:14-30, 1 Peter 4:10)

16. What are the consequences of neglecting to serve God and others? (Matthew 25:26-30, James 2:14-17)

17. What challenges or obstacles do we (you) face in serving others, and how can they be overcome? (Galatians 6:9, 2 Corinthians 12:9-10)

Wisdom to Action
Challenge

How can you tangibly serve others this week in a way that demonstrates your growing relationship with Christ? What fruit of the Spirit can you intentionally cultivate in this act of service?

Lesson 9
Reject Worldly Values

"You adulterous people! Do you not know that friendship with the world is enmity with God? Therefore whoever wishes to be a friend of the world makes himself an enemy of God."
James 4:4 ESV

THE WORLD

The term "world" in the New Testament has a variety of meanings, depending on the context in which it is used. It often refers to a system of values, beliefs, and practices that are in opposition to God's will and His kingdom. In the first section of this lesson we will provide an overview of how the concept of "the world" relates to the values of the world being in conflict with God and His values.

The Greek word *kosmos* is frequently used in the New Testament to refer to the "world" in a broad sense. While it can mean the physical universe or earth, it often refers to the moral and spiritual system that exists apart from God. In the negative sense *kosmos* represents the fallen world which is under the influence of sin, Satan, and human rebellion against God. Generally, the meanings of the word "world" in the Bible can refer to:

- a world or realm of sin
- a world controlled by Satan (organized against God)
- people opposed to God or people hostile toward God
- a human system opposed to God's purposes
- most people
- the people on earth
- the earth or universe

Worldly Values

When the New Testament refers to the world with respect to being in opposition to God, it is generally referring to:

- *Human Pride:* Elevating self rather than honoring God.
- *Materialism:* Valuing wealth, possessions, or earthly success above eternal objectives.
- *Self-Centeredness:* Seeking personal pleasure and satisfaction instead of loving God and others with all our heart, mind, body, and soul.
- *Moral Relativism:* Rejecting God's truth and living according to our own personal preferences or the cultural norms of society.
- *Rebellion Against God (sin):* Rejecting God's authority and choosing separation from Him.

These worldly values often align with personal selfish or sinful desires. They are frequently fueled by Satan's temptations.

The Nature of the World

2 Peter 1:4 *He has granted to us his precious and very great promises, so that through them you may become partakers of the divine nature, having escaped from the corruption that is in the world because of sinful desire.* ESV
1 John 3:1 *See what kind of love the Father has given to us, that we should be called children of God; and so we are. The reason why the world does not know us is that it did not know him.* ESV
1 John 5:19 *We know that we are from God, and the whole world lies in the power of the evil one.* ESV

The world, as described in these Scriptures, is a place marked by corruption, ignorance of God, and being under the influence of the evil one. Yet, God's love and promises provide a pathway for believers to rise above its brokenness.

In 2 Peter 1:4, we are reminded of the "precious and very great promises" God has given. These promises invite us to partake in the divine nature—a life of holiness and transformation. By doing so, we escape the world's corruption. This is more than a call to flee temptation. It is an invitation to embrace a life empowered by God. The world's corruption, driven by sin, cannot stop those who rely on God's promises.

1 John 3:1 further reveals the contrast between the identity of a believer and the nature of the world. As children of God we are recipients of a love so profound that it defines our very being. This identity sets us apart from the world, which neither knows nor understands God. The world's values are blind to the light of divine love, causing many believers to feel alienated at times.

Finally, 1 John 5:19 states the stark reality that "the whole world lies in the power of the evil one." This reveals the spiritual battle underlying the world's systems and values. The evil one seeks to perpetuate corruption and draw hearts away from God and His promises. Yet, those who are "from God" live under a different authority, empowered to resist the influence of darkness and walk in the light of truth.

Together, these passages underscore the believer's dual calling: to escape the world's corruption and to live as God's children. Though the world is under the control of the evil one, God's love and power equip us to stand firm, reflect His nature, and live as light in a dark world.

JESUS and the WORLD

John 3:19 *And this is the judgment: the light has come into the world, and people loved the darkness rather than the light because their deeds were evil.* ESV

John 8:12 . . . I am the light of the world. Whoever follows me will not walk in darkness, but will have the light of life. ESV
John 7:7 The world cannot hate you, but it hates me because I testify about it that its works are evil. ESV
John 8:23 He said to them, "You are from below; I am from above. You are of this world; I am not of this world." ESV
John 14:30-31 I will no longer talk much with you, for the ruler of this world is coming. He has no claim on me, 31 but I do as the Father has commanded me, so that the world may know that I love the Father. Rise, let us go from here. ESV
John 16:33 I have said these things to you, that in me you may have peace. In the world you will have tribulation. But take heart; I have overcome the world. ESV
John 18:36-37 Jesus answered, "My kingdom is not of this world. If my kingdom were of this world, my servants would have been fighting, that I might not be delivered over to the Jews. But my kingdom is not from the world." 37 Then Pilate said to him, "So you are a king?" Jesus answered, "You say that I am a king. For this purpose I was born and for this purpose I have come into the world— to bear witness to the truth. Everyone who is of the truth listens to my voice." ESV

These passages from John's Gospel reveal profound insights into Jesus' relationship with the world and His purpose within it. They describe an environment of light versus darkness and the victory He offers His followers.

Light vs. Darkness (John 3:19; 8:12)

Jesus is described as the "light" that has come into a world shrouded in darkness. The world's preference for darkness over light highlights humanity's resistance to truth, as light exposes evil deeds. Jesus offers those who follow Him the "light of life," enabling them to walk in truth and righteousness rather than be ensnared by darkness (evil).

Opposition to Jesus (John 7:7; 8:23)

Jesus testifies that the world's evil frequently provokes hatred. The world rejects Him because its values and actions are at odds with the holiness and truth He represents. Jesus distinguishes Himself from the world, declaring that He is "from above" while the world is "from below." This distinction underscores His divine origin and mission.

Authority and Obedience (John 14:30-31)

Jesus acknowledges the coming of the "ruler of this world" (Satan), yet affirms that Satan has no claim over Him. His obedience to the Father reveals His love for God and demonstrates His sovereignty over worldly powers.

Victory Over the World (John 16:33)

Jesus offers peace to His followers despite the tribulations they face in the world. His declaration, "I have overcome the world," assures believers of His ultimate triumph over sin, death, and the forces of evil.

A Kingdom Not of This World (John 18:36-37)

Jesus clarifies that His kingdom is spiritual in nature and not of this world. It operates on principles of truth and divine authority, contrasting sharply with the world's systems of power and wealth. His mission is to bear witness to the truth. He invites all who align with truth to hear and respond to Him.

Summary

Jesus' relationship to the world is one of confrontation, illumination, and redemption. He came as the light, exposing the darkness of human sin and offering the "light of life" to all who follow Him. Yet, the world's rejection of this light is evident in its hatred of Jesus and its resistance to His truth. His testimony against the world's evil is a call to repentance.

Jesus rules from a position of divine authority, untainted by the world's corruption. His obedience to the Father demonstrates a love that surpasses human understanding and sets an example for His followers to live in faithful submission to God. The world is under the control of the evil one but Jesus asserts that Satan has no power over Him. His triumph assures believers that they too can overcome the world through faith in Him.

Jesus' kingdom is not defined by physical boundaries or political power. It is a kingdom of truth, calling people out of the world's deception into the freedom and peace of divine reality. This godly foundation of truth and love stands in stark contrast to the self-centered values of the world.

Jesus offers His followers peace amid tribulation. He encourages them to stand firm in the assurance that He has already overcome the world. His life, death, and resurrection exemplify the ultimate rejection of the world's values and the embrace of God's eternal purposes. Believers are called to be lights in the darkness of the world.

THE WORLD IN CONFLICT WITH GOD

1 John 2:15-17 – Do Not Love the World
Do not love the world or anything in the world. If anyone loves the world, love for the Father is not in them. For everything in the world—the lust of the flesh, the lust of the eyes, and the pride of life—comes not from the Father but from the world. The world and its desires pass away, but whoever does the will of God lives forever. NIV

John highlights three categories of worldly values that conflict with God's will: (a) the lust of the flesh, meaning the pursuit of sinful pleasures, (b) the lust of the eyes, which is fueled by materialism and covetousness, and (c) the pride of life, meaning the quest for status, power, and self-sufficiency. Loving the world's values leads to separation from God because such values are rooted in sinful desires.

James 4:4 – Do Not be Friends with the World
You adulterous people, don't you know that friendship with the world means enmity against God? Therefore, anyone who chooses to be a friend of the world becomes an enemy of God. NIV

James equates aligning with worldly values to turning away from God's kingdom to pursue sinful ways. Being "friends" with the world compromises one's loyalty to God because the world's values are hostile and in conflict with God's righteousness.

Romans 12:2 – Do Not Conform to the World
Do not conform to the pattern of this world, but be transformed by the renewing of your mind. Then you will be able to test and approve what God's will is—his good, pleasing and perfect will. NIV

Jesus followers must resist being shaped by the world's mindset and values. The world pressures believers to adopt its ways but God calls for a life that reflects His will and values.

John 15:18-19 – The World Hates Jesus' Followers
If the world hates you, keep in mind that it hated me first. If you belonged to the world, it would love you as its own. As it is, you do not belong to the world, but I have chosen you out of the world. That is why the world hates you. NIV

Followers of Jesus are separated from the world's value system because they belong to Christ. The world opposes Jesus and His followers because His truth exposes its sin and calls for repentance.

John 17:14-16 – Do Not be *of* the World
I have given them your word and the world has hated them, for they are not of the world any more than I am of the world. My prayer is not that you take them out of the world but that you protect them from the evil one. NIV

Although believers live in the world, their allegiance is to God and His kingdom. Christians are called to remain distinct in their values and behavior while engaging the world as Christ's ambassadors.

THE GOOD NEWS

John 16:33 – Jesus Overcomes the World
I have told you these things, so that in me you may have peace. In this world you will have trouble. But take heart! I have overcome the world. NIV

Though the world opposes God's people, Jesus has won the ultimate victory over sin. Believers can have confidence in Christ's victory and His power to enable them to live faithfully in a fallen world. Believers are called to:

- *Reject Worldly Values:* Avoid conforming to the world's pursuits (Romans 12:2).

- *Pursue God's Kingdom:* Seek God's righteousness, truth, and eternal priorities (Matthew 6:33).

- *Be Salt and Light:* Shine Christ's light in a dark world (Matthew 5:13-16).

- *Love the Lost, Not the World:* Engage with people in the world to share Christ's love, but resist adopting their sinful values (1 Corinthians 9:19-23).

The world's values stand in direct conflict with God's righteousness and kingdom priorities. Jesus followers are called to reject the world's values and bear witness to God's truth as they live *in* the world but not *of* it. Christ's victory over the world gives believers the power and confidence to live faithfully for Him.

FORSAKE WORLDLY VALUES

Following Christ involves a countercultural lifestyle. True discipleship prioritizes eternal rewards over temporary earthly pleasures. We should evaluate our lifestyle choices to ensure they align with kingdom values. We can practice generosity and contentment as acts of resistance to materialism. Our goal is to be *in* the world, not *of* the world, meaning we do not want to be influenced by the values of the world or be a friend of the world!

Rejecting worldliness means we distinguish ourselves from secular values and priorities. The requirement is to focus on eternal objectives rather than earthly pursuits. Our goal is to reject the values that the world is trying to force on us. We might pray:

- I want to be in the world, not of the world.
- I do not want to be influenced by the values of the world.
- I do not want to be a friend of the world, love the world, or conform my values to the world.
- I want to set my mind on things above, not on earthly things. AMEN!

John 12:25-26 *Anyone who loves their life will lose it, while anyone who hates their life in this world will keep it for eternal life. Whoever serves me must follow me; and where I am, my servant also will be.* NIV

The teaching in this passage is a profound call to prioritize eternal values over worldly attachments. It emphasizes the necessity of self-denial, sacrificial service, and unwavering commitment to Christ. It teaches that discipleship involves a paradox. Serving and following Jesus involves forsaking worldly priorities. Those who cling to their earthly life, prioritizing comfort, safety, or selfish ambition, ultimately lose it. However, those who "hate" their life in this world (choosing Christ over personal desires) secure eternal life.

The word "hate" does not imply self-loathing or neglect. Instead, it reflects a comparison: a willingness to prioritize God to such a degree that personal desires and comfort take a distant second place. It means placing eternal values above worldly concerns.

These words invite believers to assess their priorities. What worldly attachments hinder your full devotion to Christ? Are you willing to surrender these for the sake of eternal life and divine approval? The assurance of eternal honor from God encourages believers to persevere, knowing that their sacrifices are meaningful and will be richly rewarded in eternity.

DISCUSSION QUESTIONS

1. How can we demonstrate zeal for God in our daily lives?

2. What do you think it means to "lose your life" for Christ? Has this principle ever impacted your life?

3. How can we ensure our worship (personal or corporate) remains God-centered rather than self-centered?

4. What sacrifices have you made or seen others make for the sake of following Christ?

5. How does Jesus' life and actions in these passages inspire your personal discipleship journey?

THE STORY OF DEMAS: The Danger of Loving the World

Paul's final letter to Timothy is filled with the urgency of a man nearing the end of his life, deeply concerned for the future of the gospel. In this poignant epistle, Paul writes, *"Do your best to come to me quickly, for Demas, because he loved this world, has deserted me and gone to Thessalonica"* (2 Timothy 4:9-10 NIV). These words are not merely a lament about being abandoned, but they are also a powerful warning to us about the dangers of embracing the values of the world.

Demas: A Cautionary Tale

Demas is mentioned three times in Paul's letters. In Philemon 1:24, he is listed as a "fellow worker," someone who once labored alongside Paul in spreading the gospel. In Colossians 4:14, his name appears again, though without the title or recognition of his earlier mention. By the time of 2 Timothy, however, Demas has turned away and abandoned Paul "because he loved this world."

What happened to Demas? The text doesn't specify, but Paul's words reveal that the pull of worldly values (the lure of comfort, safety, wealth, or acceptance) proved stronger than his commitment to Christ. Thessalonica, a wealthy and bustling city, may have represented the fulfillment of the desires that captured the heart of Demas.

The Nature of the World's Values

Scripture is clear that the values of the world stand in stark opposition to God's values. Colossians 3:2 exhorts believers to "set your minds on things above, not on earthly things." James

4:4 warns that "friendship with the world means enmity against God." And 1 John 2:15-17 lays bare the emptiness of worldly pursuits. The "world" in these passages is the system of values and priorities that prioritize self over God, temporary pleasures over eternal rewards, and human approval over divine truth.

Consequences of Loving the World

Demas's choice to abandon Paul and the mission of the gospel in favor of worldly pursuits serves as a sobering example. While the immediate result may have seemed minor, perhaps a more comfortable life or the avoidance of persecution, the eternal implications are devastating. Jesus warns in Matthew 6:24, "*No one can serve two masters . . . You cannot serve both God and money.*" (NIV) To love the world is to turn one's back on God, trading the eternal for the fleeting shadows of earthly success.

God's Call to Reject the World

The call to reject the values of the world is not an invitation to asceticism or withdrawal from society but a challenge to live with hearts and minds fixed on Christ. It means valuing what God values: humility over pride, service over selfishness, and truth over convenience. Jesus Himself modeled this rejection of worldly values when He resisted Satan's temptations in the wilderness (Matthew 4:1-11).

A Warning and a Call

Demas's story invites reflection: What worldly values or desires tempt us to compromise our faith or mission? Are we pursuing approval or comfort at the expense of obedience to Christ?

The story of Demas should remind us of the fleeting nature of worldly pursuits and the eternal worth of a life wholly committed to God. Jesus asks in Matthew 16:26, "*What good will it be for someone to gain the whole world, yet forfeit their soul?*" (NIV) The question is as relevant today as it was then.

Conclusion: A Choice to Make

Every believer faces the choice that confronted Demas: will we love the world or will we love God? One leads to desertion and despair and the other leads to life and eternal joy. May we learn from Demas's failure and resolve to stand firm, rejecting the seductive but hollow values of the world. Instead, may our hearts and minds be captivated by the surpassing worth of knowing Christ Jesus our Lord (Philippians 3:8).

We might ask ourselves these questions:

- What determines what I love?
- Where do I spend my time?
- Who are my friends?
- What do I really treasure?
- How do I spend my money?
- What do I get emotionally charged up about?
- Do feelings influence my words and actions?

DISCUSSION AND THOUGHT QUESTIONS

6. What do <u>you</u> think it means to "love the world" as described in 1 John 2:15-17?

7. How does the story of Demas (2 Timothy 4:9-10) illustrate the dangers of loving the world?

8. What are some practical ways to "set your mind on things above, not on earthly things" (Colossians 3:2)?

9. Why does James 4:4 describe friendship with the world as enmity with God?

10. How can we recognize when worldly values are influencing our priorities or decisions? What are the red flags?

11. How can believers encourage one another to reject the world's values and stay focused on God's kingdom? How can we help the next generation resist the pull of worldly values?

Wisdom to Action
Challenge

What worldly value or societal norm have you been conforming to without realizing it? How can you actively reject this and align yourself more closely with God's standards this week?

EXHIBIT
Man's Relationship With the World

1. God is creator, sustainer and owner of the world, but it is passing away. (Psalm 24:1; 1 Corinthians 7:31)

2. The world does not perceive God.
(John 14:17; 1 Corinthians 1:20-21; 1 Corinthians 2:14)

3. The world is a prisoner of sin and is corrupt.
(Galatians 3:22; Galatians 4:3; 2 Peter 1:3-4)

4. Satan has temporary control. (Eph 6:12-13; 1 John 5:19; John 16:33)

5. We are aliens in this world. (1 Peter 2:11)

6. Do not be a friend of the world, love the world, or conform to values of the world. (James 4:4; John 2:15-16; Romans 12:2; 1 Corinthians 3:19; 1 Corinthians 5:11; 2 Corinthians 10:2; Colossians 2:8; James 1:26-27)

7. God will judge the world and evil will be punished.
(Isaiah 13:11; Matthew 16:26; Matthew 18:7; John 12:30-31; 1 Corinthians 11:3; John 12:31; John 16:8; John 16:11; Acts 17:31)

8. The world will hate the church.
(John 15:18-19; John 17:14-15; 1 John 3:13)

9. Be shrewd in dealing with the world. (Luke 16:8-9)

10. Do not worry about what you need from the world.
(Luke 12:29-31)

11. We have victory over the world.
(2 Corinthians 10:3-6; 1 John 4:4-5; 1 John 5:4-5; 1 John 2:2)

12. We are to be light to the world.
(Matt 5:14; Mark 16:15; John 17:16-18; 1 Corinthians 8:4; 1 Peter 2:12)

Lesson 10
Persevere and Stand Firm

"It always seems impossible until it's done."
Nelson Mandela

PERSEVERANCE

Persevere Under Trial
James 1:12 *Blessed is the one who perseveres under trial because, having stood the test, that person will receive the crown of life that the Lord has promised to those who love him.* (NIV) This passage highlights perseverance as a condition for receiving God's eternal reward—the crown of life. Trials test faith, but enduring them proves our love and loyalty to God.

Suffering Leads to Perseverance
Romans 5:3-5 *Not only so, but we also glory in our sufferings, because we know that suffering produces perseverance; perseverance, character; and character, hope. And hope does not put us to shame, because God's love has been poured out into our hearts through the Holy Spirit, who has been given to us.* (NIV) Perseverance is part of the process of spiritual maturity. Suffering leads to perseverance, which shapes our character and strengthens our hope in God's promises.

Perseverance Requires Focus
Hebrews 12:1-2 *Let us run with perseverance the race marked out for us, fixing our eyes on Jesus, the pioneer and perfecter of faith. For the joy set before him he endured the cross, scorning its shame, and sat down at the right hand of the throne of God.* (NIV) Perseverance is like running a race—it requires focus, endurance, and a clear goal. By looking to Jesus as our model we can remain steadfast despite difficulties.

Persevere in Good Deeds
Galatians 6:9 *Let us not become weary in doing good, for at the proper time we will reap a harvest if we do not give up.* (NIV) Perseverance in doing good is crucial because God promises a harvest (blessings and eternal rewards) for those who remain faithful and do not quit.

Endure Hardship
2 Timothy 2:12 *If we endure, we will also reign with him. If we disown him, he will also disown us.* (NIV) Enduring hardship for Christ leads to the promise of reigning with Him. Perseverance is important in maintaining our relationship with Christ.

Persevere in Persecution
Revelation 2:10 *Do not be afraid of what you are about to suffer. I tell you, the devil will put some of you in prison to test you, and you will suffer persecution for ten days. Be faithful, even to the point of death, and I will give you life as your victor's crown.* (NIV) Perseverance in the face of persecution, even unto death, brings the reward of eternal life. This verse calls for faithfulness despite trials.

Rely on Him
Colossians 1:11 *Being strengthened with all power according to his glorious might so that you may have great endurance and patience.* (NIV) Perseverance is enabled by God's strength. Disciples are empowered by His might to endure trials and remain faithful.

Summary

These passages collectively emphasize the value of maintaining perseverance and the positive outcomes associated with a steadfast faith. In James 1:12, perseverance under trial is celebrated, promising the person who stands firm a reward in the form of the "crown of life." This indicates that enduring hardships with faithfulness leads to divine blessing.

Romans 5:3-5 speaks to the growth that comes through tribulations, illustrating that suffering produces perseverance, perseverance produces character, and character produces hope. This sequence illustrates how enduring difficulties can strengthen faith and foster spiritual development. Similarly, Hebrews 12:1-2 encourages believers to run the race with perseverance, focusing on Jesus as the ultimate example of enduring faith.

Galatians 6:9 highlights the importance of not giving up in doing good, promising a harvest of blessings if we persevere. 2 Timothy 2:12 articulates the assurance of reigning with Christ if we endure, linking perseverance directly to future glory. Revelation 2:10 reinforces this by encouraging faithfulness even in the face of suffering, promising the "crown of life" to those who remain steadfast until death.

Colossians 1:11 prays for believers to be strengthened with all power according to God's glorious might, so they may have great endurance and patience. Together these passages paint a picture of perseverance as a crucial aspect of the Christian faith, leading to spiritual growth, divine reward, and ultimate fulfillment.

STANDING FIRM

Stand Firm – Be Resolute
1 Corinthians 15:58 *Therefore, my dear brothers and sisters, stand firm. Let nothing move you. Always give yourselves fully to the work of the Lord, because you know that your labor in the Lord is not in vain.* (NIV) Standing firm involves being immovable

in faith and fully committed to serving the Lord. This assurance comes from knowing that our work for God has eternal significance. Steadfastness involves resolute commitment to God's work and His kingdom.

Unity
Philippians 1:27 *Whatever happens, conduct yourselves in a manner worthy of the gospel of Christ. Then, whether I come and see you or only hear about you in my absence, I will know that you stand firm in the one Spirit, striving together as one for the faith of the gospel.* (NIV) Standing firm includes unity with other believers and a shared commitment to the gospel. It reflects a life worthy of Christ.

Resist
1 Peter 5:8-9 *Be alert and of sober mind. Your enemy the devil prowls around like a roaring lion looking for someone to devour. Resist him, standing firm in the faith, because you know that the family of believers throughout the world is undergoing the same kind of sufferings.* (NIV) Standing firm requires alertness and resistance to Satan's attacks. Believers find strength in knowing they are not alone in their struggles.

Hold to God's Word
2 Thessalonians 2:15 *So then, brothers and sisters, stand firm and hold fast to the teachings we passed on to you, whether by word of mouth or by letter.* (NIV) Standing firm involves holding tightly to God's Word and apostolic teachings. This protects believers from false doctrines and wavering spiritually.

No Compromise
1 Corinthians 15:2 *If you hold firmly to the word I preached to you, otherwise you have believed in vain.* (NIV) Keeping the faith involves holding onto the gospel without compromise or doubt. We are to remain steadfast in our trust of God and the teachings of the gospel.

Avoid Bondage
Galatians 5:1 *It is for freedom that Christ has set us free. Stand firm, then, and do not let yourselves be burdened again by a*

yoke of slavery. (NIV) Standing firm in Christ means rejecting any return to legalism or bondage to sin. It emphasizes freedom through grace.

Be Strong
1 Corinthians 16:13 *Be on your guard; stand firm in the faith; be courageous; be strong.* (NIV) Standing firm requires vigilance, courage, and spiritual strength. It reflects a steadfast commitment to our faith.

Be Patient
James 5:8 *You too, be patient and stand firm, because the Lord's coming is near.* (NIV) Patience and standing firm are essential as believers wait for the return of Christ. This hope sustains perseverance.

Summary of Key Themes:

1. **Trials Test Faith**: Perseverance is often forged through hardships (James 1:12, Romans 5:3-5).

2. **God's Strength Enables Perseverance**: Believers rely on God's power, not their own strength (Colossians 1:11).

3. **Eternal Rewards Motivate Perseverance**: Faithful endurance brings the "crown of life" and the promise of reigning with Christ (Revelation 2:10, 2 Timothy 2:12).

4. **Standing Firm Resists Evil**: Resisting Satan and worldly temptations requires vigilance, faith, and the armor of God (1 Peter 5:8-9).

5. **Unity Strengthens Resolve**: Standing firm together in the gospel encourages perseverance (Philippians 1:27, 2 Thessalonians 2:15).

6. **Focus on Christ**: Jesus is our example and source of strength in perseverance and standing firm (Hebrews 12:1-2, John 16:33).

The New Testament repeatedly instructs disciples to persevere in trials and to stand firm in faith and righteousness. Perseverance leads to maturity and spiritual victory. Standing firm guards believers against spiritual attacks and empowers them to remain unwavering in their commitment to Christ. These qualities are essential for a Jesus follower's walk in a challenging and fallen world.

OTHER INSTRUCTIONS

There are several other terms or phrases in the Bible that convey similar meanings to perseverance and standing firm. These phrases emphasize the need for endurance, faithfulness, and steadfastness in a Jesus follower's journey:

Endure

Matthew 24:13 *But the one who endures to the end will be saved.* (ESV) Endurance is necessary to remain faithful to Christ amidst hardships.
Hebrews 12:3 *Consider him who endured such opposition from sinners, so that you will not grow weary and lose heart.* (ESV) Jesus endured opposition and suffering and believers are encouraged to follow His example and not lose faith.

Be Faithful

Hebrews 10:23 *Let us hold fast the confession of our hope without wavering, for he who promised is faithful.* (ESV) Cling tightly to faith and truth, refusing to waver. This phrase emphasizes unshakeable faith in God's promises, even when circumstances are difficult.
Revelation 3:11 *Hold fast to what you have, so that no one will take your crown.* (ESV) Holding fast involves protecting your faith and commitment to God to receive eternal rewards.
Matthew 25:21 *Well done, good and faithful servant! You have been faithful with a few things; I will put you in charge of many things.* (NIV) Faithfulness in serving God produces fruit and eternal rewards.

Beware of False Teaching

2 Peter 3:17 *You therefore, beloved, knowing this beforehand, take care that you are not carried away with the error of lawless people and lose your own stability.* (ESV) Steadfastness protects against falling into false teachings or sin.

Run and Finish the Race

Hebrews 12:1-2 *Let us run with perseverance the race marked out for us, fixing our eyes on Jesus.* (NIV) The Christian life is a race requiring endurance and focus on Jesus, who strengthens and inspires us to persevere.
2 Timothy 4:7 *I have fought the good fight, I have finished the race, I have kept the faith.* (NIV) Paul used the race metaphor to signify a life lived with perseverance and faithfulness to God's calling. Finish the race!

Focus on the Goal

Philippians 3:14 *I press on toward the goal to win the prize for which God has called me heavenward in Christ Jesus.* (NIV) Move forward with determination, persistence, and focus on the goal. *Pressing on* describes active perseverance toward the eternal reward in Christ. It reflects a mindset of never giving up.

Overcome Evil with Good

Romans 12:21 *Do not be overcome by evil, but overcome evil with good.* (NIV) Overcoming involves responding to challenges with God's power and goodness.

Summary:

- **Endure / Endurance**: Remain faithful under trials.
- **Hold Fast**: Cling tightly to faith, truth, and God's promises.
- **Be Steadfast**: Remain firm and unwavering in the face of challenges.

- **Run the Race**: Live the Christian life with focus, discipline, and perseverance.
- **Stand Firm**: In faith resist opposition and hold your ground.
- **Press On**: Push forward toward spiritual goals.
- **Faithfulness**: Be loyal and reliable in serving God.
- **Overcome**: Gain victory over sin, trials, and opposition.
- **Keep the Faith**: Maintain trust in God and His Word.
- **Victory:** Gain victory over sin, trials, and spiritual opposition through faith in Christ (Revelation 3:21 NIV).

All of these terms emphasize the necessity of remaining steadfast and faithful in the face of opposition or distractions. Together, they paint a picture of the Christian life as an active enduring journey toward spiritual maturity. A committed Jesus follower understands that perseverance and faithfulness are essential for finishing the race and bearing fruit that honors God.

BIBLICAL PARABLES/STORIES

Following are additional parables and stories that illustrate perseverance and standing firm in our faith.

The Parable of the Persistent Widow (*Luke 18:1-8*)

A widow repeatedly approached a judge seeking justice against her adversary. Though the judge was unjust and did not fear God, he eventually granted her request because of her persistence. Jesus used this parable to teach the importance of persistent prayer and unwavering faith. Perseverance reflects trust in God's justice even when solutions seem delayed. Jesus followers must persist in seeking God and not give up, especially during times of discouragement or delay.

The Parable of the Sower (*Matthew 13:1-23*)

A farmer scattered seeds on different types of soil. Only the seed that fell on "good soil" grew and produced a crop. The parable highlights the importance of spiritual perseverance. The seeds that fell on rocky or thorny ground represent people who give up under persecution or worldly distractions. Only those who persevere bear fruit. True disciples stand firm and let God's Word take deep root in their hearts, producing spiritual growth and fruit over time.

The Story of Job (*Job 1–42*)

Job experienced immense suffering, losing his family, health, and possessions. Despite his questions and struggles, Job persevered in his faith and did not curse God. In the end God restored Job's fortunes and commended his perseverance. Job's story teaches that steadfast faith through suffering honors God and can lead to restoration. When circumstances seem hopeless perseverance demonstrates trust in God's goodness and sovereignty

Peter Walking on Water (*Matthew 14:22-33*)

Peter stepped out of the boat to walk on water toward Jesus. However, when he focused on the wind and waves he began to sink. Jesus saved him and rebuked his lack of faith. Standing firm requires faith and keeping our eyes on Jesus. When we lose focus, doubt and fear can cause us to stumble.

Paul's Thorn in the Flesh (*2 Corinthians 12:7-10*)

Paul described a "thorn in the flesh" which was a persistent struggle or affliction he had to endure. Though he prayed for its removal, God told him "My grace is sufficient for you, for my power is made perfect in weakness." God's strength is displayed through perseverance in weakness. Faithful endurance under hardship reflects trust in God's grace.

The Faith of the Canaanite Woman (*Matthew 15:21-28*)

A Canaanite woman persistently begged Jesus to heal her demon-possessed daughter. Despite initial resistance, her unwavering faith persuaded Jesus to grant her request. Perseverance in faith, even when faced with obstacles, leads to blessings. Jesus followers should demonstrate steadfast faith trusting in God's mercy and timing.

The Story of Shadrach, Meshach, Abednego (*Daniel 3:1-30*)

These three men refused to bow down to King Nebuchadnezzar's golden image, even under threat of being thrown into a fiery furnace. They stood firm in their faith and God miraculously delivered them from the furnace. Standing firm in obedience to God's commands honors Him, even when facing persecution. We are called to persevere in our convictions and trust God for the results.

Summary

These parables and stories highlight perseverance and standing firm as essential aspects of the Christian life. The themes of faithfulness, endurance, and unwavering trust in God's promises emerge repeatedly. By remaining steadfast in trials and focused on Christ, we are able to produce spiritual fruit and honor Him.

THE ARMOR OF GOD

Ephesians 6:13-18 *Therefore, take up the whole armor of God, that you may be able to withstand in the evil day, and having done all, to stand firm. 14 Stand therefore, having fastened on the belt of truth, and having put on the breastplate of righteousness, 15 and, as shoes for your feet, having put on the readiness given by the gospel of peace. 16 In all circumstances take up the shield of faith, with which you can extinguish all the flaming darts of the evil one; 17 and take the helmet of salvation, and the sword of the Spirit, which is the word of God, 18 praying at all times in the Spirit, with all prayer and* *supplication. To that end keep alert with all perseverance, making supplication for all the saints.* ESV

Meaning and Key Points

Ephesians 6:13-18 is part of Paul's description of the armor of God, which equips believers to stand firm against spiritual opposition. The instructions are to:

1. **Take up the whole armor of God**: This emphasizes the need for total spiritual preparation, not partial reliance on some of the weapons to stand against the devil's schemes.

2. **Stand firm**: Scripture repeatedly stresses the importance of perseverance and holding fast in the face of spiritual challenges.

3. **Pray in the Spirit**: Prayer is necessary to empower the armor and foster dependence on God. This means aligning our prayer with the Spirit's guidance and will.

4. **Use the Armor Components**:

    - **Belt of Truth**: Living in and speaking the truth of God's Word secures our spiritual foundation.
    - **Breastplate of Righteousness**: God's righteousness protects our hearts and guards us against sin and guilt.
    - **Gospel of Peace (Shoes)**: Readiness to proclaim and live in the peace of the gospel helps believers remain stable.
    - **Shield of Faith**: Faith deflects the attacks of doubt, fear, and temptation.
    - **Helmet of Salvation**: Assurance of salvation guards the mind against discouragement.
    - **Sword of the Spirit**: God's Word is the only offensive weapon listed and is capable of countering lies and spiritual deception.

Standing firm is not passive but requires an active commitment to spiritual discipline and reliance on God's strength.

The Core Message

The central message of this passage is that believers are engaged in a spiritual battle and must rely on God's provision and power to stand firm. This passage aligns with other New Testament teachings like 1 Peter 5:8-9 where it tells us to "*Resist the devil, standing firm in the faith.*" James 4:7 says to "*Submit yourselves to God. Resist the devil, and he will flee from you.*" These passages share a focus on spiritual vigilance and dependence on God's power rather than on human strength.

Paul draws on the familiar image of a Roman soldier's armor to illustrate spiritual preparedness. This context resonates with his audience who understood the importance of each piece of equipment for both defense and offense in battle. Paul's audience would have recognized "spiritual forces," making his call to stand firm against evil particularly relevant and urgent.

Practical Application

1. **Daily Readiness**: Start each day by mentally and spiritually "putting on" the armor through prayer and meditation on God's Word. Know key Scripture verses in order to be prepared to respond to questions and challenges ("the Sword of the Spirit").

2. **Guarding the Heart and Mind**: Be vigilant against influences that undermine righteousness or peace. Filter out cultural messages using biblical truth to discern the lies of the enemy and the culture.

3. **Faith in Action**: Use faith to counter doubt, fear, and discouragement.

4. **Gospel Sharing**: Actively live out and share the peace of the gospel with others.

5. **Prayer Discipline**: Develop a consistent prayer life, seeking the Spirit's guidance and intercession.

6. **Relationships**: Build accountability relationships for encouragement to stand firm.

MOTIVATION

Priorities can be a problem for a Jesus follower who is struggling in their faith walk. Are your priorities right? Is Jesus the number one priority in your life? If your faith is not a high priority in your life you will probably find it difficult to persevere and stand firm when challenges or difficulties occur.

It may not be easy for you in this season of your life to proclaim the supremacy of God. It may even be difficult to praise His holy name if you are struggling to keep your head above water! Or you may simply be worn out and find it hard to keep the main thing the main thing.

You may need a vision of God that will motivate you to transform your relationship with Him. That generally means getting back to the basics: actively and intentionally seeking to renew your mind through prayer, worship, the study of God's Word, and the power of the Holy Spirit. This should be done in community where others can help and encourage you.

There is only one way to be transformed and be made more like Christ. We must get on our knees crying out to God for transformation. I don't think it will occur in any other way. We must humble ourselves before God and beg Him to have mercy on our miserable lives. God must become central in our life:

> **Mark 12:28-30** *Of all the commandments, which is the most important? 29 "The most important one," answered Jesus, "is this: 'Hear, O Israel, the Lord our God, the Lord is one. 30 Love the Lord your God with all your heart and with all your soul and with all your mind and with all your strength.'"* NIV

We cannot have other gods or idols in our lives. In Jesus' day the major issue was the worship of idols and wooden statues. Today, it is self, money, wealth, power, status, careers, hobbies, etc. Nothing is to be more important than God. Jesus must become the central reality of your life.

DISCUSSION AND THOUGHT QUESTIONS

1. Why is perseverance essential to the life of a Jesus follower?

2. What are some challenges for <u>you</u> that make it difficult to stand firm in your faith? How can you overcome these challenges?

3. Can you share a time when perseverance in your faith led to spiritual growth or blessing? Have you personally experienced verses like Galatians 6:9 ("Let us not grow weary of doing good")?

4. What role does prayer play in helping you personally persevere and stand firm? Explain.

5. Why is endurance compared to running a race in the New Testament (e.g., Hebrews 12:1-2)?

6. How can believers find hope in trials while standing firm in their faith?

7. How does fellowship with other believers help Christians persevere and stand firm?

Questions Focused on the Armor of God

8. Why is the "whole armor of God" necessary, and what happens if we neglect any part of it?

9. What are some practical ways to take up the "shield of faith" when facing doubts or fears?

10. How can the "Sword of the Spirit" (God's Word) be used effectively in spiritual battles?

11. How can modern distractions or cultural values hinder believers from standing firm?

12. What practical steps could you take this week to "put on" the full armor of God?

Wisdom to Action
Challenge

In what area of your faith are you feeling weak or tempted to compromise? What specific strategy can you implement to stand firm and persevere in your commitment to Christ?

Embrace a Biblically Centered Life!

Transformation Road Map

Primary Takeaways

1: True discipleship requires unwavering commitment to Christ, characterized by a growing relationship with Him, active learning, and a transformative dedication to a Christ-like lifestyle. This commitment is driven by love for God and it involves continual spiritual growth, obedience, and seeking after God's heart in all aspects of life.

2: Pleasing God should be an overarching goal of a committed disciple. It is demonstrated through faith, sacrificial living, spiritual growth, bearing fruit, seeking God's will, shunning evil, and performing acts of kindness which reflect a heart aligned with His will and purpose.

3: We must develop an enduring faith in our commitment to Christ which is expressed through obedience and love which leads to sacrificial living, spiritual growth, and a life dedicated to God's purposes. This faith is about actively growing in relationship with Christ and learning and applying God's Word in order to shape our lifestyle and service to others.

4: Being a committed follower of Christ involves a total surrender and submission to His Lordship, prioritizing Him above all else. We are to express devotion through love, obedience, and a life that reflects His teachings.

5: Taking up our cross signifies a willingness to deny oneself, sacrifice personal desires, and endure hardship for the sake of following Jesus. This requires a dedication to a Christ-like lifestyle and a deep personal devotion to God.

6: We must strive to be a living sacrifice which means offering ourselves fully to God, resisting conformity to worldly values, and undergoing a transformation of the heart and mind to align with His will.

7: Committing to spiritual growth is an ongoing pursuit of the Jesus follower. It requires actively learning and applying God's Word, growing in a relationship with Christ, and bearing fruit in every good work.

8: Serving others and producing fruit are essential expressions of a committed faith, demonstrating a growing relationship with Christ through acts of love, compassion, and generosity. This commitment is about a heart transformed by God's love, resulting in a life that honors Him through service to others.

9: Rejecting worldly values is essential for a Christian, requiring a life that pleases Him rather than seeking human approval or conforming to sinful patterns. We are to shun evil and embracing goodness and light.

10: Persevering and standing firm in our faith requires a Jesus follower to resist worldly influences, remaining steadfast in our commitment to Christ, and actively pursuing spiritual growth.

Embrace a Biblically Centered Life!

Leader Guide

This Guide is designed to give a leader answers and additional information to effectively lead a discussion of each lesson in this book.

Tips For Leading

We recommend that you begin a group discussion by reading an appropriate Scripture. It may be one that you will cover in the material or another related passage you have chosen. This will do several things:

- Allow time for everyone to get settled.
- Remind everyone of the subject and bring their minds to a common focus.
- Provide a transition from the previous activity.

Additional ice-breakers are usually not necessary, but if your group is new or members don't know each other well, you could have someone give their testimony/story at the beginning of each week. If you sense that the group needs additional focus before you begin with the discussion, conduct a <u>short</u> discussion about the themes of the lesson or ask about the meaning of a particular term associated with the lesson.

Goals

The discussion should center around the questions in the lesson. But remember that each person in your group has different goals and is at a different place in his or her Christian walk. Jesus may be an old friend to some but a new acquaintance to others. The dynamic of the group will vary depending on the nature of the participants.

Your goal as the Leader should be to foster understanding and familiarity with Scripture. For new believers or participants who are not comfortable with the Bible, your goal should be to help them get over that hurdle and begin to seek knowledge and understanding from His Word.

More mature participants will probably dig deeper to find personal meaning and understanding. They may particularly desire to discuss application questions and issues.

Prayer
Unless you have an outstanding person of prayer in your group, you as the leader should wrap up your discussion time with prayer that specifically reflects the discussion and the themes, purpose, and focus of the lesson.

Answers to Questions:

Lesson 1 Being a Committed Disciple
DISCUSSION QUESTIONS: Pleasing God

1. Yes, in Mt 3:17 God says He is well pleased and in John 8:29 Jesus says He pleases the Father.
2.

Romans 12:1	being a living sacrifice
Romans 14:17	being righteous, a peacemaker, and having "joy in the Holy Spirit"
Philippians 4:18	being generous
Colossians 1:10	living worthy of the Lord: bearing fruit and knowing God
Colossians 3:20	being obedient to parents (honoring them)
Hebrews 11:6	having faith
Hebrews 12:28	being thankful and worshipping authentically (acceptably)
Hebrews 13:21	exercising our spiritual gifts
Galatians 1:10	being a servant of Christ
1 Thessalonians 2:4	having a heart fully committed to the gospel
1 John 3:22	being obedient
1 Timothy 2:2-3	living in godliness and holiness
1 Timothy 5:4	caring for family

3.

Ro 14:23	having faith (no serious doubts)
John 15:5	abiding (remaining) in Christ
Gal 2:20	living by faith in Jesus
1 Cor 15:10	living fervently by the grace of God

4.
Yes, the scriptures never indicate that a Jesus follower will not have difficulties or suffer. But that does not mean all followers suffer, or suffer in the same degree.

EXERCISE:
1. Hold on to the Vine.
A committed disciple is expected to:
1. Maintain vital connection with Christ.
2. Submit to God's pruning process.
3. Produce visible spiritual fruit.
4. Live in active obedience.
5. Participate in kingdom work.
6. Demonstrate authentic faith through actions.
7. Experience ongoing spiritual growth.
8. Impact others for Christ.

2. Fear God and keep His commandments
1. Fear God: (a) Maintain a proper reverence and awe of God; (b) Acknowledge God's sovereignty and authority; (c) Demonstrate respect through worship and attitude.
2. Keep God's Commandments: (a) Obey God's instructions faithfully; (b) Prioritize following God's will; (c) Live according to biblical principles.
3. Recognize Life's Purpose: (a) Understand that serving God is our primary duty; (b) Accept that life without God lacks true meaning; (c) Acknowledge that following God gives purpose to life.
4. Live with Accountability: Remember that God will judge all actions.
5. Maintain Integrity: Live honestly, knowing God sees everything.
6. Exercise Wisdom: Apply God's truth to daily decisions.
   a. Regular self-examination of motives and actions.
   b. Consistent study and application of God's Word.
   c. Intentional development of godly character.
   d. Active participation in worship and humble service to others.
   e. Careful attention to both public and private conduct.
   f. Ongoing commitment to spiritual growth.

3. Total Allegiance and priority.
A committed disciple will:
1. Exhibit love and compassion towards others.
2. Acknowledge personal shortcomings and seek growth.
3. Be willing to sacrifice personal comforts for the sake of following Christ.
4. Actively pursue a relationship with Jesus through obedience.
5. Prioritize eternal values over material possessions.
6. Embrace a radical commitment to discipleship that transforms his life.

4. Guard your hearts (inner self).
While **Proverbs 4:23** is the most explicit instruction to guard the heart, the Bible as a whole emphasizes this principle by teaching believers to protect their hearts from evil, to fill their hearts with God's Word, and to rely on the Holy Spirit for help in guarding against influences that can lead to sin or straying from God's path. Guarding the heart, then, is a biblical principle central to spiritual health and integrity.

While **Philippians 4:7** does not directly tell believers to guard their hearts, it promises that God's peace will guard our hearts when we focus on Him.
In **Matthew 15** The heart influences our behavior. Although the command is not explicitly guarding the heart, Jesus words highlight why protecting the heart from evil influences is crucial.

5. Be alert, stand firm
1. Be watchful and remain alert to spiritual dangers.
2. Stand firm in the faith by adhering to biblical truths.
3. Act with courage and maturity in their convictions.
4. Draw strength from God to face challenges.
5. Do everything in love, ensuring that love governs all actions.

DISCUSSION AND THOUGHT QUESTIONS

1. There is a daily cost and commitment of discipleship. Being a committed disciple means putting Jesus' priorities above my own comfort and preferences. It includes daily choices to follow His teaching even when it's difficult or goes against family and friends.
2. Faith impacts everyday life choices and priorities. Commitment to Christ affects everything from how I spend my money (ensuring I tithe and give generously), to how I use my time (prioritizing prayer, Bible study, and service), to how I treat others (showing patience and love even in difficult situations). It means viewing all my resources as belonging to God and being accountable for how I use them. I am to be a good steward in all facets of my faith.
3. It helps to identify common struggles in order that group members support each other in overcoming obstacles. The biggest challenges may be the constant distractions of social media, the pressure to conform to secular values at work, or the temptation to prioritize comfort over commitment. One might struggle with maintaining spiritual disciplines when life gets. It may be hard to balance various commitments while keeping Christ first.
4. Self-examination helps identify genuine markers of discipleship versus surface-level religion. Authentic commitment shows up in heart attitudes, not just actions. It's reflected in genuine love for others, a desire to grow closer to God, and a willingness to serve even when no one is watching. It's about relationship with Jesus, not just following rules or maintaining appearances.
5. Regular prayer and Bible study are essential, along with being part of a small group for accountability. Serving others regularly helps keep faith active and growing. Writing in a spiritual journal can be helpful.
6. Initially, I [the author] thought being a disciple was mainly about following rules and attending church. Over time, I've learned it's about a deep, transformative relationship with Jesus that affects every aspect of life. It's about becoming more like Christ in character and allowing His love to flow through me to others. I've realized it's a lifelong journey of growth and surrender. And it's not always easy because life gets in the way.

Lesson 2 Total Commitment
DISCUSSION QUESTIONS

1. It means prioritizing Jesus above all else, even cherished relationships, while still loving others. It means prioritizing Christ's teachings and mission, even when it conflicts with family expectations.
2. Giving up unhealthy habits, material wealth, certain toxic relationships, or worldly values, may be required.
3. Living counter to cultural norms, enduring criticism, sacrificing comfort, denying personal desires, or making sacrifices and enduring hardships for the sake of following Christ.
4. Practicing generosity, living simply, and trusting God for provision, if necessary.
5. Surrendering personal plans and earthly ambitions for God's purpose often brings deeper fulfillment and peace.
6. It prevents shallow faith and prepares believers for challenges. Some new believers may think all their problems are going to disappear because of their new spiritual status.
7. It calls for humility, sacrifice, and a focus on eternal rewards, not on worldly material wealth.
8. Staying focused on Christ and His mission; avoiding distractions that pull us away. Discipleship is work. It means prioritizing God's will over personal desires and giving up selfish ambitions.
9. Past sins, comfort zones, personal relationships, or worldly ambitions can be tempting. The Kingdom's work is vital and time-sensitive, requiring undivided attention. Looking back can be a distraction and can cause a disciple to lose focus. There is also the danger of fleshly desires being strengthened.
10. Technology, materialism, focus on self, and societal pressures can divert our attention from our spiritual life. Today's culture promotes self-indulgence, making it difficult to respond with total attention to Christ.
11. A lukewarm faith lacks zeal, purpose, or meaningful engagement with God's mission.
12. Materialism, busyness, and societal indifference to faith can dampen zeal. Being active in your faith community can be a great help.
13. The warning is sobering but also reflects God's desire for restoration and fellowship.
14. Work, relationships, personal habits: Any area where God is not prioritized or obedience is compromised needs re-evaluation.
15. It includes loving others, forgiving, serving, and prioritizing God's will over personal desires.
16. Cultural pressures, busyness, and personal struggles can hinder total commitment.

Lesson 3   Choose Enduring Faith
DISCUSSION AND THOUGHT QUESTIONS

1. Spiritual decisions cannot be avoided. Doing nothing is a choice. Not choosing the good alternative often means you have chosen the bad.
2a. Education, career, marriage, lifestyle, health, location of home, children.
2b. Does God exist? Who is Jesus? What does that mean for me?
3. "If you don't know where you are going, any road will get you there." The Bible suggests we "count the cost" for any important decision. If the decision is about faith:

    (1) following the King requires serious thoughtful consideration.

    (2) remember Christianity will never be a majority movement; there will always be push-back.

4. In the Sermon on the Mount Jesus had been describing the narrow road, He just didn't refer to it in those terms. He had been discussing: a) the beatitudes, b) salt and light, c) murder vs. anger, d) adultery and divorce, e) oaths, f) an eye for an eye, g) love your enemies, h) giving to the needy, i) prayer, j) fasting, k) love of money, l) worry and anxiety, m) judging others, and n) seeking Him. **Pretty serious stuff!**
5. The wide road!
6. It represents the high moral path for the Jew – the Law put the Jew on a narrow path to becoming God's people by defining moral right/wrongs.
7. There is an exclusive nature to entering the Kingdom. One does not enter eternity without going through the narrow gate.
8. It's "easy" and more popular. There are a lot more people traveling with you. There are few rules, requirements, or restrictions. You can do want you want. You may feel entitled, and there is often instant gratification. There is unrestricted access to hell.
9.

a) I must commit to living pursuant to the teachings of Christ. I have no say in the rules.

b) It does not involve the approval of others. There is only Christ and His requirements.

c) I cannot put myself first. It goes against the normal way of secular living of elevating self.

d) There is no other gate – no other option.

e) The narrow way requires submission, self-discipline, and intentional love toward others. I may want to reject that.

10.

a) Only through Him can anyone get thru the gate to receive life.

b) Jesus is the only Savior! (John 14:6 and Acts 4:12)

c) The narrow road will be difficult, challenging, and may require followers to stand firm on their beliefs.

11.

a) There is a cost.

b) We must surrender and submit.

c) It requires genuine heart commitment.

d) Ethical values are not desirable to a degenerate heart.

e) There can be cultural pressures, fear of sacrifice, or misunderstanding the

cost/joy of discipleship.
12. Somebody would likely choose the *narrow path* in order to:
   a) Receive joy, blessing, assurance, peace, rest, etc.
   b) Avoid bad consequences of the wide road.
   c) Desire for eternal life.
They might choose the *wide road* because:
   a) They made no choice. Apathy and laziness simply prevented choosing.
   b) They were in active rebellion against God/Jesus.
   c) They were strongly influenced by unbelieving friends or associates.
   d) No one ever explained the Gospel effectively.
13. An important "requirement" of being on the narrow path is that the Jesus follower is obedient to the salvation requirements of the faith.
14. There is a paradox of finding freedom and fulfillment through surrender and discipline (Matthew 11:28-30). Salvation is not free – Jesus paid the price; therefore, He has the right to establish heart requirements for those who will follow Him.

Lesson 4 Lordship, Surrender, and Submission
DISCUSSION AND THOUGHT QUESTIONS

1. Is He the one and only god in your life? Is He sovereign in your life? Do you recognize Him as creator and sustainer of your life? Do you acknowledge everything you have is His?
2. This is a good question! If you were arrested for being a Jesus follower is there enough evidence to convict you? Are you in a small group? What would they say about you? What would co-workers say?
3. Do you ever insist on doing it on your own or in your own way? Do you ask God about big decisions before charging ahead?
4. Jesus has the power and authority in my life; I submit to the will of God; I am obedient to Jesus' teachings and commands; I am submissive to Christ.
5. n/a
6. Trust or dependence on another can be scary.
It is easier to trust in myself because I know what I will do.
I may not like what Jesus wants to do.
7. Yes . . . It is the key to a real or true relationship with Christ!
a) It's always under the surface of many spiritual requirements.
b) It may impact quiet time, worship, relationship, abiding, obedience . . .
8. n/a
9. Example: Slave . . . One who is completely subservient to a controlling influence.

Believers in the Bible repeatedly referred to themselves as the Lord's slaves: Ro 1:1; 1 Cor 7:22; Gal 1:10; Eph 6:6; Php 1:1; Col 4:12; Titus 1:1; James 1:1; 1 Peter 2:16; 2 Peter 1:1; Jude 1; and Rev 1:1. The NT reflects the perspective of commanding believers to submit to Christ completely – not just as hired servants or spiritual employees, but as those who belong to Him totally. We are instructed to obey without question or complaint. Jesus is our Master! This is a fact we acknowledge every time we call Him "Lord." We are His people, called to obey and honor Him.

The slave's sole duty was to carry out the master's wishes. Those who claim Christ, but continue to live in disobedience betray their profession of faith. 1 John 1:6 speaks to this situation: "If we claim to have fellowship with him yet walk in the darkness, we lie and do not live by the truth." NIV
Parallels between biblical Christianity and 1st century slavery:
(A) Exclusive ownership: Ro 5:18-19; Eph 2:1-3; 1 Pet 1:18-19; Rev 5:9; Ro 6:14-18; 1 Cor 7:23; Titus 2:14; Gal 5:24; Col 4:1; Rev 3:12, 22:4
(B) Complete submission: 1 John 2:3; 1 Pet 1:2; Ro 12:1; 1 John 3:22; 1 Cor 6:20
(C) Singular devotion: Mk 12:30 Mt 6:24; Ro 7:5-6, 6:11-18; 1 Thess 1:9; Heb 13:21; 2 Cor 5:9; Col 1;10; 1 Thess 4:1; Ro 14:18
(D) Total dependence: Mt 6:31-33; 1 Tim 6:8; Php 4:19; 2 Cor 9:8, 12:9
(E) Personal accountability: Ro 14:12; 2 Cor 5:10; 2 Tim 4:8
10. n/a
11.
DO: Give up control, trust in Him, turn it over to him, hold onto the Vine, and wait on Him.
NOT DO: Take control and do it in my strength, worry, and charge ahead without thinking or praying.
UNIQUE/SPECIAL CIRCUMSTANCES:
a. VOLUNTARY: For a Christian the act **must be voluntary**. One must recognize and accept that Jesus is God, which means He is worthy, my Creator, and my Savior. I acknowledge Him as sovereign, faithful, and true.
b. FREE WILL: The interesting thing about Lordship is that not only do I choose to accept it, I can also refuse it or take it back at any time I wish.
12. a) I live and operate in the power of God; b) I am satisfied with God's results; c) I do not feel responsible or guilty about the results, d) I am effective, e) I achieve God's result and not mine, f) It allows me to abide.
13a. Am I fighting giving up control in my life? Why?
13b. Who is really in charge/control of my life?
14. n/a

Lesson 5 Take Up Your CROSS
DISCUSSION AND THOUGHT QUESTIONS

1. Relinquishing self-centered desires in favor of God's will. It means responding to the sacrifices, requirements, and priorities required to live as a disciple.
2. Embracing sacrifice and identifying with Christ's suffering, including living counter-culturally.
3. True life is found in surrender, not in self-preservation or worldly gain.
4. Pursuing materialism, fame, or power at the expense of one's relationship with God. It may imply living in a sinful condition.
5. By prioritizing His Word, prayer, community, and courageously standing on the truth.
6. A deep love for Christ, gratitude for my salvation, and an eternal reward.
7. Living with a heart of surrender and holding possessions loosely. Rejecting worldly values.
8. Following Jesus demands total allegiance because of the eternal stakes

involved. The sin problem must be solved. We must "work out" our salvation. It requires honest self-reflection and renewed dedication to Christ.
9. Encourage them through prayer, accountability, and shared experiences. Help others face their difficulties and challenges.
10. Abiding involves consistent prayer, obedience, and reliance on Christ.
11.
a. What are God's standards for my life?
b. What does He expect from me?
c. How am I to live as if matters?
d. What does God want me to do? Do I really want to know?
e. How do I measure up?
12. Challenges often refine faith, leading to greater reliance on God.
13. It emphasizes dependence on Christ rather than personal effort.
14. It highlights the futility of human effort without divine empowerment.
EXHIBIT QUESTION: Total commitment, total dedication, steadfast and unwavering, and actively doing something.

Lesson 6 Be a Living Sacrifice
Discussion Questions:

1. Giving fosters dependence on God and alignment with His purposes. Sacrificial giving demonstrates trust in God's provision and love for others.
2. It requires focus, humility, and faith, even in difficult times. We can cultivate a lifestyle of continual praise through prayer, reading God's Word, meditation, and gratitude. Our minds are renewed because our praise aligns our thoughts with God's truth and fosters spiritual transformation.
3. By surrendering all aspects to His control we demonstrate that obedience produces transformation and dedication to God.
4. Faith gives us strength to trust and obey. Even trials can strengthen our faith and commitment because they refine our character and deepen our dependence on Him.
5. Serving others, forgiving, and giving generously! Love mirrors Jesus' selflessness and obedience to the Father.
6. Mercy reflects His character and relational priorities. We can practice mercy by empathizing and forgiving just as Christ forgave us.
7. It requires time, focus, and surrender. It can transform lives into a living sacrifice by fostering dependence on and intimacy with God.
8. It requires boldness, time, and love. It reflects our commitment to God because it fulfills His mission and glorifies Him. It also is the proper response to the Great Commission (Matthew 28:18-20).
DISCUSSION AND THOUGHT QUESTIONS
9. Living with intentionality and aligning my words and actions with God's will.
10. STEPS: Immersing oneself in Scripture, prayer, and the godly influences of other disciples.
11. Materialism, individualism, and ungodly temptations.
12. Through prayer, meditation, studying Scripture, and seeking wise counsel.

13. It creates in the mind of the Jewish reader the importance of the subject/activity being discussed.

It associates the suggested activity with laws that had been required in the Old Testament, giving them a similar flavor, helping to highlight the importance of obedience.

14.
PRIORITY: My #1 priority must be my relationship with Christ!
OBEDIENCE: In order to be right with God, my life must be dedicated and acceptable to God (Ro 12:1).
SIN: I must get rid of any and all sin from my life (1 Sam 7:3).
SEEKING: I must seek first His kingdom and His righteousness (Mt 6:33).

15.
SPIRITUAL ACTS OF WORSHIP: Others see and are pointed to God.
GIFTS: They relieve and meet the needs of others.
PRAISE: My words reflect the nature of my relationship with Him.
SPIRITUAL SACRIFICES: Reflect my spiritual growth.
FAITH: I stand firm.
LOVE: I love God (Great Commandment).
MERCY: The Great Commandment also tells us to love our neighbor.

16.
General: How am I doing? Do I really take these seriously?
For me: n/a

17. Suggestions: (a) Address the weakest area first. (b) Find someone to hold you accountable for your commitments.

Lesson 7 Commit To Spiritual Growth
DISCUSSION QUESTIONS:
Spiritual Growth
1. Spiritual growth can be reflected in a deeper love for God and others and greater obedience to God's Word.
2. Barriers may include distractions, sin, apathy, lack of discipline, or discouragement. Overcoming them requires intentionality, prayer, accountability, and reliance on God's strength.
3. God's Word provides wisdom, correction, and encouragement, shaping our hearts and minds to align with His will (Psalm 119:105; 2 Timothy 3:16-17).
4. Community and fellowship provides encouragement and opportunities to learn and serve together, as seen in Acts 2:42-47 and Hebrews 10:24-25.

<u>Knowing God's Word</u>
5. The Bible is not just a historical book but a dynamic divine tool that speaks to our hearts today, revealing truth and transforming lives. Studying it allows God's Word to work powerfully in us.
6. Meditation involves deep reflection and internalization of God's Word, enabling it to shape our thoughts, attitudes, and decisions. It fosters a closer relationship with God and accumulates spiritual wisdom.
7. Memorizing Scripture provides quick access to God's truth, strengthens our resolve to resist sin, and offers encouragement in moments of weakness or trial. It can provide answers quickly when one is under duress to make a decision.
8. The Bereans exemplified diligence, enthusiasm, and discernment in studying Scripture. Their example should encourage us to prioritize consistent and thoughtful engagement with God's Word. It should be the primary source

for gaining understanding and wisdom.
9. Faith is built over time on hearing and understanding God's Word. Studying Scripture reassures us of God's character and His faithfulness, helping us stand firm in difficult times.
10. Distractions like busyness, complacency, or lack of discipline can hinder Bible study. Overcoming them requires setting priorities, scheduling dedicated time, and praying for a hunger for God's Word.
Psalm 119
11. Cultivating such love involves regular reading, studying, and reflecting on its truths. Knowledge brings understanding and understanding produces wisdom. Love often produces a deep desire to learn.
12. God's Word anchors us with unchanging truth, offers hope in trials, and reassures us of His presence and promises, leading to inner peace and resilience.
13. The psalmist reflects on God's Word as a source of joy, wisdom, comfort, and strength. Believers can share testimonies of how Scripture has impacted specific areas of their lives.

Lesson 8   Serve Others and Produce Fruit
DISCUSSION QUESTIONS

1. Others will see fruit and praise God.
2. True faith naturally results in good works as the fruit of its existence. If there is no fruit one must question the spiritual condition of the follower.
3. Superficial faith lacks genuine transformation and submission. Thus, it will likely lack obedience.
4. Individualism, materialism, and busyness can distract from discipleship. Intentional focus on Christ helps overcome these challenges.
5. Through encouragement, accountability, mentoring, and shared study of God's Word.

DISCUSSION QUESTIONS: Parable of the Talents
6. Talents represent gifts, time, skills, or opportunities. Participants might identify specific resources or skills God has given them.
7. God values faithfulness over outcomes. Success is measured by obedience and effort, not comparison to others.
8. Neglect leads to missed opportunities and accountability before God. It's a call to actively engage in His work.
9. By serving in church, sharing the gospel, mentoring others, or using our skills for God's kingdom.
10. Serving and sharing the gospel often involve stepping out of comfort zones and trusting God with the results.

11. Praying for each other, serving together, or mentoring one another. Being friends!

12. Participants can share personal experiences and encourage each other to act on them.

DISCUSSION AND THOUGHT QUESTIONS

13. Jesus modeled servant leadership and taught that serving others reflects His character. Serving is not optional but an essential part of following Him. Serving others demonstrates humility, love, and obedience to Jesus. By serving, we mirror Christ's example and bring glory to God. It completes the second half of the Great Commandment.

14. Jesus taught that whatever we do for others, especially the "least" among us, we do for Him. Serving others is an act of worship to God. It is a way to honor God because He identifies with those in need. When we serve with a pure heart, He is glorified.

15. God has entrusted each person with gifts, time, and opportunities to serve. Identifying these gifts requires prayer, self-reflection, and community input. We can identify our gifts by recognizing what we're passionate about, asking for feedback from others, and stepping out in faith to serve where there is a need.

16. Jesus warns that neglecting to use what God has entrusted to us can lead to stagnation, missed opportunities, and spiritual loss. When we neglect to serve, we miss the joy of participating in God's work, and our faith can become empty and unfruitful.

17. Challenges such as pride, busyness, discouragement, or lack of resources can hinder service. God's grace empowers us to persevere. We can overcome obstacles by depending on God's strength, remembering our purpose, and seeking encouragement and help from other followers.

Lesson 9   Reject Worldly Values
DISCUSSION QUESTIONS

1. By prioritizing worship, protecting our spiritual integrity, and speaking publically against practices that dishonor God.
2. MEANING: Surrendering personal ambitions or comforts to serve Christ fully.
3. Focus on prayer, Scripture, and aligning worship practices based on Jesus and His Word, rather than social or feel good topics.
4. Examples could include financial giving, career changes, or enduring persecution for being faithful.
5. His example of zeal, sacrifice, and service motivates believers to live with a similar commitment.

DISCUSSION AND THOUGHT QUESTIONS

6. The term "world" refers to the system of values and desires that oppose God's will, characterized by lust, pride, and selfish ambition. In modern

culture, these create temptations for Jesus followers. A committed Jesus follower would reject "loving the world" (prioritizing earthly success, pleasures, or approval over a relationship with God).

7. Demas may have left Paul because worldly values pulled him away from God's mission. Demas might have been drawn by comfort, safety, or material gain, warning against similar distractions in our own lives.

8. Daily practices like prayer, Bible study, and serving others help believers focus on eternal values. We should intentionally prioritize spiritual growth, seeking God's will in decisions, and regularly engaging in spiritual disciplines.

9. Worldly values often conflict with God's commands and the dangers of trying to serve two masters can be overwhelming. A committed Jesus follower should see this as a call to loyalty, understanding that divided allegiances weaken faith and obedience.

10. Red flags are neglecting spiritual commitments, seeking approval over integrity, or justifying sinful behaviors . A committed Jesus follower should examine their choices in light of Scripture and seek help and accountability from trusted Christians.

11. Building strong relationships within a faith community helps believers remain steadfast and aligned with God's values.

12. Discuss with young disciples practical ways to model godliness, teach biblical truths, and equip them for spiritual battles. Mentoring, leading by example, and providing a solid foundation in Scripture can guide others to choose God's values over those of the world.

Lesson 10   Persevere and Stand Firm
DISCUSSION AND THOUGHT QUESTIONS

1. Scriptures like James 1:12 and Romans 5:3-5 emphasize the refining and maturing power of perseverance. Perseverance builds spiritual maturity, strengthens character, and deepens reliance on God.

2. We should identify any external pressures (persecution, cultural opposition) and internal struggles (doubt, fear). A committed Jesus follower overcomes these challenges by trusting God, leaning on Scripture, and seeking support from the Christian community.

3. n/a

4. Remember passages like Luke 22:39-46 (Jesus in Gethsemane) or Paul's exhortation to "pray without ceasing" in 1 Thess. 5:17. Prayer aligns the believer's will with God's desires, strengthens resolve, and invites divine intervention.

5. Running a race requires discipline, focus, and effort. Perseverance is like a race because it demands sustained commitment and focus on Jesus as the ultimate goal.

6. Review Romans 8:28 and 2 Corinthians 4:16-18, which point to God's

sovereignty and eternal perspective. A Jesus follower finds hope in knowing that trials are temporary and purposeful, leading to eternal rewards. Disciples who experience tough times can lean on the Christian community.

7. Hebrews 10:24-25 stresses the importance of encouragement and accountability. Fellowship provides support, shared wisdom, and reminders of God's truth during struggles. Christian community can be a great asset for those struggling with spiritual challenges.

Questions Focused on the Armor of God

8. Each piece of armor is vital for spiritual readiness. Neglecting any piece leaves one vulnerable to specific spiritual attacks in the ignored area.

9. Recalling God's past faithfulness and declaring His promises aloud strengthens faith. Talk to brothers or sisters who have strong faith and obtain their help and perspective.

10. Use specific verses that counter common spiritual struggles. Jesus used Scripture to resist temptation (Matt. 4:1-11), modeling its power in combating lies. **LEADER:** You may want to bring to the discussion a list of God's promises that address common life problems. For example:

Isaiah 41:10 (NIV): "So do not fear, for I am with you; do not be dismayed, for I am your God. I will strengthen you and help you; I will uphold you with my righteous right hand."

Jeremiah 29:11 (NIV): "For I know the plans I have for you," declares the Lord, "plans to prosper you and not to harm you, plans to give you hope and a future."

Romans 8:28 (NIV): "And we know that in all things God works for the good of those who love him, who have been called according to his purpose."

11. Typical challenges are busyness, materialism, entertainment, and relativism.

12.

Study Scripture: Regularly read and meditate on the Bible to understand God's truth. This can help combat lies and confusion. Be open and honest in your relationships, ensuring that your words and actions align with the truth of God's Word. Regularly engage with the Bible, not just as a reader but as a learner who seeks to apply its teachings in practical ways.

Confession and Repentance: Regularly confess sins to God and seek forgiveness. This helps maintain a clear conscience and a right standing before God. Actively seek to live according to God's standards by making choices that align with His will, such as showing kindness, integrity, and love toward others.

Share Your Faith: Engage in conversations about your faith and the peace that comes from knowing Christ. This can reinforce your own beliefs and encourage others. Actively seek to be a peacemaker in your relationships and community. This can involve resolving conflicts and demonstrating grace.

Prayer: Develop a consistent prayer life in which you bring your doubts and struggles before God. Trust Him to provide strength and guidance. Establish a daily routine for prayer, including adoration, confession, thanksgiving, and supplication. Seek God's guidance in your struggles. Pray for others who are struggling, fostering a sense of community and support. Ask others to pray for you as well.

Helmet of Salvation: Regularly meditate on what it means to be saved and the implications of your identity in Christ. This can strengthen your assurance and confidence. Be intentional about what you allow into your mind (media, entertainment, conversations, etc.) and focus on thoughts that align with God's truth.

Community Support: Engage with a local church and a small group for accountability, encouragement, and fellowship. Sharing struggles with others can provide support and insight. Consider talking to a pastor, mentor, or trusted friend about your struggles. They can provide wisdom and support as you navigate challenges.

Appendix A
We Reap What We Sow!

In a number of his proverbs, King Solomon suggests that doing what is right is to be preferred over evil. King Solomon was known world-wide for his great wisdom. He wrote and recorded many proverbs recognized for their practical insight and wisdom. He described the nature of righteousness as being immovable and that it will stand above evil.

Is your desire for doing what is "right" rooted deeply or is it planted in shallow soil that can easily be washed away? Solomon indicated that the wicked would ultimately be overthrown and that the righteous would survive because their character had roots that were deep and impossible to dislodge.

Solomon argued that it was better to be on the side of the righteous. The reasoning is the same as the man who builds his house, business, or life on rock versus sand. If we build on sand (questionable ways) then our hopes and plans will never stand up against the storms of life. If we build on rock (character, commitment, and obedience) our plans will hold firm.

We do reap what we sow and if we sow badly because we have rejected the wise counsel of friends or our core values, we will reap the negative consequences. Those who think they know everything frequently reject wisdom and follow their own plans and schemes. It has been said that those who insist on following their own foolish ways will often end up choking on them.

Choices produce consequences
which direct the course of life.
Consequences shape lives.
Therefore, count the cost!

Embrace a Biblically Centered Life!

Free PDF
MAKE WISE DECISIONS

[Get the ebook version for 99 cents]

Consequences Shape Lives.

This book discusses the nature of decisions and explores eight essential questions to make better decisions.

You are a few decisions away from transforming your life. You can make better decisions! This resource has sections on what makes a poor decision, questions to ask yourself, traps to avoid, short and sweet decisions, the wise decision framework, and twenty ways to be wise. It also has a handy decision-making checklist. (12 pages)

Free PDF: https://getwisdompublishing.com/resource-registration/

Kindle ebook for 99 cents: https://www.amazon.com/dp/B0FG8NC53J

Ebook

Free PDF

Ten Steps to Wise Choices

Timeless Wisdom. Practical Tools. Lasting Impact.

Embrace a Biblically Centered Life!

Free PDF
Life Improvement Principles

[Get the ebook version for 99 cents]

> ### *You can live your best life!*
>
> Welcome to a journey of discovery! In case you have forgotten, your actions have consequences. Unlock your potential! This book (60+ pages) provides the overview of all our strategies and wisdom principles to live your best life. You *can* transform your life! Get your wisdom-based roadmap to a better life and unlock all the possibilities for growth and success.
>
> **Free PDF:** https://getwisdompublishing.com/resource-registration/
>
> **Kindle ebook for 99 cents:**
> https://www.amazon.com/dp/B0FG883KZM

Ebook

Free PDF

Make it your life goal to be the best you can be!

Discover Wisdom and live the life you deserve.

Embrace a Biblically Centered Life!

What Next?
Continue Your Journey

Continue Study in the *Jesus Follower* Series
The Jesus Follower Bible Study Series
https://www.amazon.com/dp/B0DHP39P5J

Be Challenged by the *OBSCURE* Series
The *OBSCURE* Bible Study Series
https://www.amazon.com/dp/B08T7TL1B1

Tackle Wisdom-Driven Life Change
Apply Biblical Wisdom to Live Your Best Life!
"Effective Life Change"
https://www.amazon.com/dp/1952359732

Know What You Should Pray
Personal Daily Prayer Guide
https://www.amazon.com/What-Should-Pray-Personal-Journal/dp/1952359260/

Decide to be the Very Best You Can Be
The Life Planning Series
https://www.amazon.com/dp/B09TH9SYC4

You Can Help:
SOCIAL MEDIA: Mention The Jesus Follower Bible Study Series on your social platforms. Include the hashtag #jesusbiblestudy so we are aware of your post.

FRIENDS: Recommend this series to your family, friends, small group, Sunday School class leaders, or your church.

REVIEW: Please give us your honest review at
https://www.amazon.com/dp/1952359759

Embrace a Biblically Centered Life!

The OBSCURE Bible Study Series
Continue your journey through the hidden
wisdom of Scripture with the OBSCURE Series.

Blasphemy, Grace, Quarrels & Reconciliation: The lives of first-century disciples.
This book presents Joseph of Arimathea, Joanna, Ananias, Hymenaeus, and Cornelius (a centurion). It illustrates the nature and challenges of life as a first-century disciple.

The Beginning and the End: From creation to eternity.
This book has four lessons from Genesis and four from Revelation covering creation, rebellion, grace, worship, and eternity. God is leading us to worship in the Throne Room.

God at the Center: He is sovereign and I am not.
This book examines the virgin birth, worship, prayer, the sovereignty of God, compromise, and trust. God is at the center of all these stories. He is at the center of our lives.

Women of Courage: God did some serious business with these women.
This book examines the lives of Jael, Rizpah, the woman of Tekoa, Tabitha, Shiphrah, and Lydia. These women exhibit great courage and faithfulness. God used them in amazing ways.

The Beginning of Wisdom: Your personal character counts.
In this book we find courage, loyalty, thankfulness, love, forgiveness, and humility. Personal character counts. Decisions have consequences. Wisdom will help us stand firm in our faith.

Miracles & Rebellion: The good, the bad, and the indifferent.
God hates sin and loves to heal the faithful. The rebellion of Korah, Haman, and Alexander compare to the healing stories of Aeneas, a slave girl, and the crippled man at Lystra.

The Chosen People: There is a remnant.
This book concentrates mostly on Israel in the Old Testament, but also covers some interesting subjects as Lucifer, Michael the archangel, and Job's wife.

The Chosen Person: Keep your eyes on Jesus.
The focus is on Jesus and the superiority of Christ. We investigate Melchizedek, the disciples on the road to Emmaus, Nicodemus, and the criminal on the cross.

WEBSITE: http://getwisdompublishing.com/products/
AMAZON: www.amazon.com/author/stephenhberkey

Embrace a Biblically Centered Life!

Life Planning Series

Read these books if you want to live a better life.
The primary audience for this series is the secular self-help market, but the concepts are Christian based.

CHOOSE FAITH	**For the spiritual seeker and those with spiritual questions.** *Your Spiritual Guidebook For Questions About Religion, God, Heaven, Truth, Evil, and the Afterlife.* https://www.amazon.com/dp/1952359473
CHOOSE CORE VALUES	**Core values will drive your life.** https://www.amazon.com/dp/195235949X
<td colspan="2" style="text-align:center"> **Other Titles in the Life Planning Series** </td>
<td colspan="2"> CHOOSE Integrity </td>
<td colspan="2"> CHOOSE Friends Wisely </td>
<td colspan="2"> CHOOSE The Right Words </td>
<td colspan="2"> CHOOSE Good Work Habits </td>
<td colspan="2"> CHOOSE Financial Responsibility </td>
<td colspan="2"> CHOOSE A Positive Self-Image </td>
<td colspan="2"> CHOOSE Leadership </td>
<td colspan="2"> CHOOSE Love and Family </td>
<td colspan="2" style="text-align:center"> LIFE PLANNING HANDBOOK A Life Plan Is The Key To Personal Growth https://www.amazon.com/gp/product/1952359325 </td>

Go to:

https://www.amazon.com/dp/B09TH9SYC4

to get your copy.

Embrace a Biblically Centered Life!

Personal Daily Prayer Guide
Prayer Resource and Journal

This is a great resource to kick-start your prayer life!

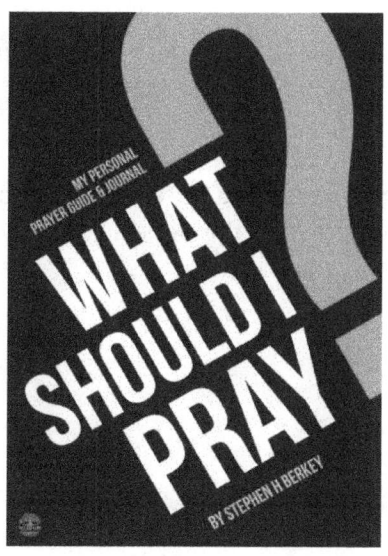

Know what to pray.
Pray based on Bible verses.
Strengthen your prayer life.
Access reference resources.
Pray with eternal implications.
Write your own prayers if desired.
Organize and focus your prayer time.
Learn what the Bible says about prayer.
Find encouragement and advice on how to pray.
Reduce frustration and distraction in your prayer time.

Get your copy today!

https://www.amazon.com/What-Should-Pray-Personal-Journal/dp/1952359260/

Acknowledgments

My wife has patiently persevered while I indulged my interest in writing. Thank you for all your help and assistance.

Our older daughter has been an invaluable resource. She has also graciously produced our website at
www.getwisdompublishing.com

Our middle daughter designed the covers for most of my books, but I gave her a vacation on this Series. We are very grateful for her help, talent and creativity.

Notes

1 "*Lord*", Easton's Bible Dictionary
2 "*Lord*", International Standard Bible Encyclopedia
3 "*Atonement*", Fausset's Bible Dictionary
4 "*Sacrifice*" , International Standard Bible Encyclopedia
5 "*Atoning Sacrifice*" (at-one-ment), Nelson's Bible Dictionary

About the Author

Steve attended church as a child and accepted Christ when he was 10 years old. But his walk with Jesus left a lot to be desired for the next 44 years. In 1994 he "wrestled" with God for some period of months and in September of that year totally surrendered his life to Jesus.

In 1996 he was so driven to study God's Word that he attended the Indianapolis campus of Trinity Evangelical Divinity School (Chicago) to earn a Certificate of Biblical Studies. His hunger for God's Word led him to lead and write all his own Bible studies for his small group. He has been a Bible study leader for the past 25 years.

After 25 years as an actuary, and 20 years as an entrepreneur, he began his third career as an author in 2020, when he published The OBSCURE Bible Study Series. The Jesus Follower Bible Study Series was completed in early 2025. He is a member of The Church at Station Hill in Spring Hill, TN, a regional campus of Brentwood Baptist (Brentwood TN).

"Get Wisdom Publishing is dedicated to being the trusted source of wisdom-driven books that inspire growth, guide decisions, and empower readers to live with purpose and fulfillment."

Embrace a Biblically Centered Life!

Contact Us

Website: www.getwisdompublishing.com

Email: info@getwisdompublishing.com

Facebook: Get Wisdom Publishing

Author's Page:
www.amazon.com/author/stephenhberkey

Amazon's Jesus Follower Bible Study Series page:
https://www.amazon.com/dp/B0DHP39P5J

"Go beyond devotionals.
Experience biblical wisdom in action!"

www.ingramcontent.com/pod-product-compliance
Lightning Source LLC
Chambersburg PA
CBHW060320050426
42449CB00011B/2568